in
Local Government

by

Kieron Walsh

General Editors: Michael Clarke and John Stewart

in association with the Local Government Training Board

Marketing in Local Government

Published by Longman Information & Reference,
Longman Group Ltd, 6th Floor, Westgate House,
The High, Harlow, Essex CM20 1YR, UK.

First published 1989
Reprinted February 1992
Reprinted 1993, May 1994

British Library Cataloguing in Publication Data
Walsh, Kieron
Marketing in local government -
(Longman local government training
board series. Managing local government; 3).
1. Great Britain. Local authorities.
III. Stewart, John, *1929 Mar. 19-*
352.041

ISBN 0-582-02553-2

Typeset by Tradeset Photosetting Ltd, Welwyn Garden City, Herts
Printed and bound in Great Britain by Antony Rowe Ltd, Chippenham, Wiltshire

Contents

Other titles in the series

Human Resource Management in Local Government
by *Alan Fowler*

Managing Beyond the Local Authority
by *Rodney Brooke*

Organising for Local Government: a local political responsibility
by *John Barratt and John Downs*

Strategic Planning
by *Ian Caulfield and John Schultz*

Understanding the Management of Local Government: its special purposes, conditions and tasks
by *John Stewart*

Editors' Foreword

This book is one of the first in a new management series launched by the *Local Government Training Board* to be published by *Longman Group UK Ltd*. The series is designed to help those concerned with management in local government to meet the challenges of the next few years. It is based on the belief that in no period has it been so important for local authorities to have effective management.

The impact of government legislation is clear. Each local authority has to review its management, if it is to achieve an effective response. But the challenge is much deeper. In a changing society, new problems and issues demand from local authorities a capacity to respond in new ways. Local authorities have to become closer to their public as customer and citizen; resources have to be managed to achieve value in service; the requirement on all authorities is to achieve effective management of the changes which are taking place.

Effective management requires effective management development. The series is designed to aid the management development of present and future officers — and councillors. It is designed to be *used* by the reader in a variety of situations. While we hope that the books will be used on local government management courses we hope that they will have a much wider use.

They can be used by individuals or groups of managers or as the basis of seminars within authorities. However, the series will truly be a success if it becomes regarded as resource material for use in the business of management itself. We hope that the ideas discussed and the experience pooled will be a stimulus to more effective management.

The series is based on two principles. The first is the need for even greater emphasis on developing effective management in local government and the constant search for improvement. The second is that effective management must take account of the nature of local government. Need for effective management has already been stressed: the case for a separate series particular to local government is based on our second principle.

There are plenty of management books. What we have set out to produce is a series geared to the particular needs of local government. We would want to argue that those concerned with management in local government should draw on as wide a range of general experience as possible. Furthermore we would also want to argue that proper account is taken of the special purposes, conditions and tasks of local government. These books will help the manager to do just that. In publishing them we are not pretending that there is *one right way* to manage a local authority. Rather, we are exposing ideas and questions to help fashion the most helpful and effective approach to the local situation.

The first books in the sequence serve both to introduce the series and to highlight some of the key issues facing management in local authorities. The series will be extended by covering other issues of contemporary concern which require to be tackled if management — and the health of the local authority — is to be improved.

Michael Clarke, Director, Local Government Training Board
Professor John Stewart, Institute of Local Government Studies

Part I
Towards public service

1 The public service orientation

Key points

- ▲ *Local bureaucracy as the mass production of services*
- ▲ *The analogy with the mass production of manufactured goods and the reasons for failure of the mass production strategy*
- ▲ *The need for a public service orientation in local government*
- ▲ *The importance of quality, choice, access and participation in the provision of public services*
- ▲ *Marketing as a contribution to the development of a more responsive public service*
- ▲ *The plan of this book*

Local government provides public services on a huge scale. Just as manufacturing industry mass produces material goods, so the local authority mass produces public services. Henry Ford discovered in the production line a means of mass producing consumer goods, which, through the reduction of cost, led to widespread access to motor cars. Since the invention of the production-line, factory production has made a huge array of manufactured goods widely available. The development of large scale bureaucracies for the provision of public services provides an analogy with the development of mass production for manufactured goods. The development of efficient bureaucratic systems has been no less important in the development of the modern world than mass production. Local authorities have provided, through the development of professional bureaucracies, the means of delivering roads, education, housing, libraries and a host of other services on a huge scale. Bureaucracy has served to make uniform services widely available. Like the production-line the bureaucracy has been highly efficient, but, as with mass production that efficiency has been attained by sacrificing flexibility, variety and responsiveness. The emphasis has been upon quantity of service rather than quality or variety, which will be increasingly important in the future.

Henry Ford eventually found that the Model T, which enjoyed huge popularity, lost to the competition from the organisationally more sophisticated General Motors, which produced a choice of cars to meet the preferences of different sections of the market. More generally, in the case of manufacturing industry there has been a search for greater flexibility and variety as people become less satisfied with uniform products. Local government is now finding that its single model for the delivery of services, the professional bureaucracy, is being questioned, and that alternative means of delivering services are being sought. What once gave great satisfaction, the provision of schools, houses, and other services on a huge scale, is now taken for granted or even found to be unsatisfactory. There are demands that new services, such as economic development, be created to meet new problems. There are demands that established services, like housing and education, should be provided in new ways, and should meet new needs. Local government must move from the era of the mass production of standard services to the flexible production of non-standard services. It needs to be flexible both in the services that it provides and the way that it provides them.

My aim, in this book, is to contribute to the thinking that is now taking place about the nature of public service management. In local government this thinking has been developed most explicitly in the search for a 'public service orientation', which will embody a revised and renewed expression of the values that underpin local government. There is a search for a new approach to the design and delivery of public services. Local authorities are not alone in their search for new approaches to the delivery of service. Private sector companies have become increasingly concerned with the pursuit of 'excellence' and with 'closeness to the customer', and a renewed emphasis on quality of service is playing a growing role in business strategies. The concern for the public service orientation recognises the need for two specific requirements to be met by modern local authorities – that they be public and that they provide service. It shows the desire to take local authorities forward into a more flexible, responsive future. The concepts that are embodied in the marketing approach can have a role to play in the development of that more responsive future.

Marketing is part of the public service orientation, because if local authorities wish to respond more effectively to the concerns and needs of the public they will need to know what those needs and concerns are. Marketing developed in the post war years in manufacturing industry as products became more diverse and demand more sophisticated. Manufacturers had to respond to the demands of the market because they could no longer sell whatever they made but had to try to make what they could sell. The development of a more sovereign consumer meant that manufacturing industry had to devote increasing energy to finding out what it was that people wanted. As local authorities come to provide more sophisticated and varied services in a more complex environment, so they, too, will need to develop the skills of marketing.

From growth to restraint and beyond

The priority of local authorities from 1945 until the early 1970s was the development of public services on a massive scale. Change was rapid and extensive, in housing, education, social services, town planning and development, public transport and other services. The need for services and the form that they should take were not seen as contentious matters. There was a broad consensus on the need for more services and in the belief that they were provided more effectively by public sector organisations. There were, certainly, arguments, for example about the merits of comprehensive education, but they were not significant enough to lead to any questioning of the agreement that the public services should be expanded. The agreement on the need for public services extended to an agreement on the way that they should be delivered.

Local authorities developed the following characteristics in the post-war years:

▽ Bureaucratic: the organisation of the local authority was dominated by detailed rules and procedures which were intended to produce uniformity, equity and predictability in the way that it dealt with people.

▽ Large and centralised: large size was seen as necessary in order to attain economies of scale. The size of the organisation created a gap between those who actually delivered services and those at the centre of the organisation. Power lay with those at the centre.
▽ Self-sufficient: the normal approach was for the local authority itself to employ those who were to deliver the service. There was little reliance on other agencies. As a result local authorities became very large scale employers. In many instances the local authority became the largest employer in the locality.
▽ Professionally dominated: professional experts controlled local authorities. There were the lawyers and accountants at the centre and the individual services were each dominated by specific professional groups. Professional judgement was dominant in deciding on the nature of services and the method of service delivery.
▽ Concerned for structure: management was conceived in terms of structures of organisation. The pre-occupation with getting the structure of committees and departments right is vividly illustrated by the Bains Report. There was much less concern for what took place within that structure – for the culture and process of the organisation, and for effective management systems.

Growth in expenditure became the normal expectation and spending rose from £866 million in 1948–49 to £11 570 million in 1974–75, which, even with inflation, was a huge increase. Change was made relatively easy because the funds were available to make it possible. Local government was, certainly, responsive but there was a tendency to assume that services could only be developed with the injection of large amounts of new money. The availability of money led to the adoption of large scale approaches to problems that took little account of the human problems that were created, for example, by high rise housing. There was a faith in economies of scale and big was seen as beautiful. Local authorities developed systems that were able to deliver standardised services with great efficiency and reliability. The faith in large scale operation and uniformity of service has been eroded since the mid-1970s. The combination of financial constraint and growing public and central government dissatisfaction with local authority services has led to a search for new forms of organisation and new approaches to the delivery of services.

We are at an early stage in the development of the 'new management' of local government, but its dimensions are already clear. In contrast to the traditional approach to the management of the local authority, the new management is:

▽ Responsive: aiming to meet a range of divergent and changing needs through differentiated services that recognise the need for change.
▽ Small and decentralised: the search is for ways to gain the advantages of being small within large organisations, and to place authority and responsibility with those who deliver services. Power is being shifted from the centre to the edge of the organisation
▽ Cooperative: working with other organisations, public and private, statutory and voluntary, and recognising the links between the work of the local authority and that of other agencies and individuals. Much of the management of local authorities will, in future, be concerned with the creation and maintenance of service networks.

▽ Consumer-controlled: allowing the consumer/client/citizen to influence the services that are provided.
▽ Concerned with process: local authorities are increasingly concerned with the culture and systems of the organisation, with process as much as with structure.

The change is slow and halting, and the pace of development varies from authority to authority, as does the approach, but the direction is clear. Authorities are thinking hard about their roles. The initiatives are taking many forms:

▽ Campaigns promoting the local area and the authority such as the Glasgow's Miles Better and Bradford's Bouncing Back campaigns.
▽ Decentralisation initiatives in Islington, Tower Hamlets, Walsall and many other authorities.
▽ Some authorities are using regular opinion polls to gauge public satisfaction with the services they provide.
▽ A number of authorities have devoted effort to the development of a strong corporate identity.
▽ There have been attempts to involve the users in the management of the service, for example, in housing and social services.
▽ Local authorities have attempted to provide more information to the public in a form that is easier to understand than the traditional jargon of the public authority.
▽ There have been the development of complaints systems that genuinely try to resolve grievances.
▽ Forming private companies to develop services.
▽ Developing cooperative arrangements with the private sector.
▽ Delegation of financial control to cost and profit centres.

Many initiatives and developments by authorities are detailed in 'Good Management in Local Government' and in 'Getting Closer to the Public', published by the Audit Commission and the Local Government Training Board.

The large bureaucratic systems that were built up in the post-war years will not change quickly. They were not established in order to enhance change and adaptability, but to ensure stability, continuity and uniformity. Nor should the virtues of efficient bureaucracy be ignored, for, as the Arden Report on Hackney has shown, systems and procedures are vital. The result of the lack of a good bureaucratic system, as Arden says, is:

> . . . lack of budgeting, lack of planning, lack of monitoring, lack of information, lack of consideration of the effects of policies . . . lack even of authority itself, bouncing instead from crisis to crisis, short-term problems engendering short-term solutions, resulting in attention diverted from long-term plans and problems, in turn re-engendering short-term crisis, a constant vicious cycle, which it seems no-one has been able to break out of. (Arden – Interim Report p. xi)

We must ensure, in the search for new approaches, that we do not destroy the virtues of the old. A good bureaucracy has the virtues that are in part its weaknesses in that it does not bend with every breath of wind. Just as we would wish to preserve the virtues of the small within the large, so we would want to preserve the values of bureaucracy in more responsive forms of organisation.

The pressure for change is now great. The Government is proposing to introduce a range of measures that will transform the way that local authorities work.

- ▽ The Community Charge, a standard, per capita, tax on everyone of eighteen and over, is to replace the domestic rates, the non-domestic rate is to be replaced by a national uniform business rate, and the grant system is to be revised.
- ▽ Local authorities are to be compelled to put a range of services out to competitive tender and to operate internal trading accounts.
- ▽ In education a national curriculum is to be introduced, schools are to be allowed to opt out of the local education authority, and are to operate open enrolments, budgets are to be delegated to schools, the ILEA is to be abolished, and polytechnics and some higher education colleges are to be taken out of local authority control.
- ▽ In housing tenants are to be allowed to opt out of local authority control, and rent from other landlords.
- ▽ Urban Development Corporations are being established and policy towards the inner city is being revised.
- ▽ The world of social services is changing rapidly and there may be further changes following the Griffiths Report.
- ▽ The conduct of local authority business will change following the Widdicombe Report.

The Government's intention is to increase choice, efficiency and accountability. It can be debated whether the policies that are being adopted will provide the results that are wanted, but radical change in the management of local authorities are inevitable. Budgets and employment levels may decline rapidly as services are contracted out to the private sector or schools and housing tenants opt out of local authority control. The agenda is daunting, and it is clear that unless, and perhaps even if, local authorities change the Government will change them.

The impetus for change does not arise only from Government pressure. Local authorities themselves recognise the need to develop new approaches and methods of management. Traditional approaches are less effective in the more complex world that we now face. It is not only the Government but also the local authorities themselves that want to improve the way that they operate.

Choice, quality, access and participation

The public service orientation is a guiding philosophy for local authorities trying to meet the challenge of developing new and more responsive patterns of organisation. It is based upon the simple idea that local authorities should provide services *for* and *with* people not simply *to* them. It is not for professionals alone to decide that a service is needed, how it is to be provided, and whether needs have been met; the wants of citizens, and their judgements on the adequacy of service are at least as important as those of the experts. The public service vision is of an organisation that is open, responsive and involved with those it serves and learns from them. The greater the level of change the more public organisations and managers need to have the capacity to learn. The public are seen not as an irritant in the body bureaucratic, but as an integral part of the authority's service approach. The emphasis is upon what each part of the organisation can contribute to the quality of service. The organisation's activities can be seen as involving a chain of quality and, for each activity, one needs to ask:

What does the activity contribute to the service that the authority is trying to provide?

The danger of bureaucracy is that things continue to be done because they always have been done. Bureaucracy can be an excellent mechanism for continuing to do the same thing. The vision of better public service must be expressed in the systems, structure, processes and culture of the organisation.

The organisation's culture, the set of attitudes, beliefs, ideas, understandings, procedures and everyday rules that make an organisation what it is, must express the vision of better public service. Cultures are what give organisations their character. It is the culture that we describe when we answer the question, 'What sort of organisation is this?' Consistent, positive organisational cultures are difficult to develop and take a great deal of time to change, because they become ingrained in the everyday operation of the organisation and the experience of its members. We cannot easily change attitudes and approaches that have become almost part of our personalities and our everyday understandings and actions. The notion of public service does not wholly reject a bureaucratic culture, but tries to retain its virtues of impartiality, equitable treatment of cases and clear records and procedures, while not sinking under its weight or succumbing to its timetable. It emphasises decentralised responsibility, autonomy and accountability within a framework of co-ordination and control. We need to be small and large at the same time.

The organisational culture that developed in the period of local government growth after the war was internally focused, developing systems and procedures that would deliver a uniform service efficiently. Such systems are subject to great strain as they try to respond to new demands. As Roger Harrison put it:

> During the past few decades, as our needs and wants became more differentiated and unpredictable, systems have had to become more complex in the attempt to respond to customer wants, and they have predictably becomes less reliable as a result.

We are at a point where the whole approach to organising for public service is changing to an emphasis upon customer satisfaction. The difficulty will be preserving efficiency and reliability while undergoing change and producing a responsive service.

The customer emphasis has four dimensions:

▽ quality
▽ access
▽ choice
▽ participative control

Quality is not the same as grade; a service may be low grade, because there is the level of service we have decided we want, but good quality. There is no point in criticising a perfectly good bicycle because it's not a Rolls Royce. A good service of the right quality is one that is fit for its purpose and that meets the service specification. The determination of the quality of services is particularly difficult, because, unlike material goods, we cannot test them after production and before delivery. Specifying and developing quality is a key task for the future. Quality will depend upon the skill and understanding of the staff. This is why staff training is so important for public services and can be seen as the internal marketing of the organisation to its own staff. But quality is not a matter for the producer alone;

the quality of service delivered may not be the same as received, which can only be judged by the client. If we would know the quality of service we must seek out the public's views and listen to them so that we can see services as people experience them. Quality is not an absolute concept but is a matter of debate with the user or consumer.

There is little point in a service existing if those who need or want it cannot get access to it. Effective distribution is much more difficult for public services than for manufactured goods. Access to services is determined by:

- ▽ Geography: for example poorly sited offices or inadequate transport will prevent access.
- ▽ Physical features: public service offices can deter through the lack of parking spaces, unwelcoming reception areas, daunting public buildings or poor signposting.
- ▽ Time: times of office opening can make services difficult to use.
- ▽ Psychological and social: we may feel uncomfortable in the face of staff and systems that are large and impersonal.
- ▽ Language and culture: it is difficult for many people to get access to service simply because they cannot understand the organisation.
- ▽ Information: we may lack access simply because we do not know about a service.

Access is most difficult for those who have the greatest need. People with disabilities who may be highly dependent upon public services often face considerable access problems. People from ethnic minority groups are often deterred from using a service because they do not know about it or because of cultural differences. Women with young children may find it difficult to make use of public services because of the times of opening or the physical design. Old people often do not know of the public services that might be available to them or are unwilling to use them. There may be multiple barriers to service, with one compounding another; linguistic and cultural barriers may, in turn, create psychological barriers.

Choice is fundamental, not incidental. Some would see individual choice as destructive of local government, and certainly, in the growth of local services, choice has often been limited. But a public service that is valued will allow individual choice, and will attempt to maximise it:

> . . . our reason for respecting wants and choices is that that is how we show our respect for the people whose wants and choices they are. . . . (Rhodes 1987)

The local authority is a system for collective choice, but there is a great danger of the tyranny of the mandate. Certainly the constraints of collective provision will limit the degree of individual choice, for there is the possibility that the collective result of everyone pursuing their own best interests may be that everyone is worse off. If we all try to drive our cars on the road at the same time none of us will be able to move. Collective choice will be prior to but should not be destructive of individual choice.

Participative control means that people must have control over the services that they need or have an interest in. If they do not feel that services belong to them they are not likely to be willing to defend them. The dominance of professionalism and producer control often leave people feeling that they have little part to play in the provision of services. If often appears that doctors would like us to be ill on a planned and pre-arranged basis, and I have often heard it said that universities would be fine places to work in if only there were no students. It is as if services are produced for the sake of the producers and not for the benefit of the consumer. The public services have sometimes encouraged dependence and taught helplessness. The future is likely to be more one of people taking control of their own lives. Representative democracy, especially when it generates little active support, is not a strong enough justification for action. It needs to be supported by participatory democracy, with those who have a stake in a service taking an active interest in its production and management.

The development of access, choice, quality, and participation poses a challenge to local authorities to move from a production to a service orientation. The traditional values of citizenship and caring need to be enhanced by consumerism. Some will see this as destructive of local government, by introducing the market and exchange into what should be decisions based on need. The assumption on which this book is based is that an effective organisation must be close to those who use, buy or receive its services, whether it is a commercial organisation or a local authority.

The consumer perspective

The words which we have to describe the recipients of the local authority's services are inadequate. This has long been so, and has been recognised, for example, in social services where there has been much debate over whether 'client' adequately describes the recipient of social services. 'Consumer' and 'customer' may be seen as inappropriate terms because they have private market overtones that are out of place in the public service. Public services are different:

▽ Many of the services that a local authority provides are not delivered to individuals, still less to individuals who pay for them and consume them.
▽ We may force individuals to receive a service in their own or the general interest.
▽ We may act on behalf of others, for example in enforcement and inspection services such as environmental health.
▽ We may act on behalf of the public as a whole, for example in providing police services or street lighting.
▽ We may provide 'public goods', such as clean air or an unpolluted environment, from which it is impossible to exclude people and in which the consumption of one individual will have no impact on that of others.

Many services are provided to individual, identifiable, consumers who may pay individually, for example in housing or the collection of trade refuse. But local government does much more than produce goods and services that are exchanged for money in transactions between identifiable individuals. It embodies the collective and community aspects of our lives.

The local authority is constituted for more than the delivery of services, and the debate over the proper description of the recipients of services is a debate about values and purposes, not simply the logistics of distribution. The local authority is not simply an institution for the efficient delivery of service, it is a government in its own right, and within the constraints of statute. It is elected to have a care for the local area that goes beyond the sum of the individual services that it delivers; it has an independent right to tax and must choose between competing priorities. The notion of the individual consumer is not enough. We must also encompass a broader notion of the consumer with power and with obligations, and the collective aspects of consumption. Local authorities must develop the responsibilities of citizenship both in their own management and in the local community.

The word consumer needs to be used with care, for the relationship between consumer and producer in public services cannot be reduced to the exchange of goods for money. The link is more intricate and complex than that. But the burden of this book is that the consumer perspective is part of a public service orientation in government. Marketing is, in turn, necessary to the consumer perspective.

Marketing

There are many definitions of marketing. The British Marketing Board defines it as:

> The management process responsible for identifying, anticipating and satisfying consumer requirements profitably.

The definition I prefer is that of Philip Kotler, who bases it upon the concept of a transaction, which is the 'exchange of values between two parties'. He says that:

> Marketing is specifically concerned with how transactions are created, stimulated, facilitated and valued. (Kotler 1982)

Marketing is more than selling, and it is much more than selling what you can make. The limitation of Kotler's definition is in his notion of two parties to the exchange. Many parties may be engaged in the exchange process particularly in the case of the public services. But this definition is valuable in focusing upon the dynamic and creative nature of marketing, and in seeing it as a process, not just a set of techniques.

Marketing developed in the private manufacturing sector. It became necessary as products became more complicated and diverse, and demand more subtle and varied. Companies had to have greater knowledge of what consumers wanted and consumers needed a deeper understanding of the products that were being produced. Gaining a competitive edge became dependent upon marketing skills as much as production costs, as Japanese industry showed. In the late 1960s and the 1970s there was a growing interest in the marketing of services. Since the late 1970s marketing thinkers have been turning to the problems of applying marketing concepts in non-profit and government organisations. Some British local authorities have been appointing marketing officers and managers over the last few years. Their focus has, so far, been narrow, largely upon leisure, sales and public relations work. In the United States the developments have gone further, and marketing is widely accepted in public sector organisations.

I shall argue that marketing is more a management approach and process than a set of specific techniques. Certainly there are very specific, and highly technical, skills needed, but they are not the whole of, or even the bulk of, the approach that local authorities might adopt. There is a danger of marketing imperialism, the hiring of professional experts who introduce the marketing approach. I will argue that marketing needs to be more widely developed than that, as part of general organisational recognition of the need to be close to the customer.

The plan of the book

The next chapter of the book is concerned with the difficulties of applying marketing concepts in the management of local authorities. There are a number of arguments typically put forward to support the argument that marketing approaches are not applicable to the world of local government. I shall propose that these arguments do not invalidate the concepts of marketing when applied to local government, but mean that they must be applied with care and taking into account the specific context in which they must operate. I shall then go on to outline the basic concepts of marketing, arguing that there are essentially two types of marketing — strategic marketing and consumer marketing. The third chapter is concerned with the ideas of strategic marketing and will discuss the meaning of market segmentation, market position and the marketing mix. This chapter will also contain a discussion of the nature of market research. The next chapter will consider the consumer perspective and I will argue that, if we are to apply marketing effectively in the local authority we must have a much clearer understanding of the psychology of the consumer of local services.

The second part of the book is concerned specifically with the application of marketing concepts in local government. I shall start off by arguing that local authorities are concerned with the provision of services rather than material goods and that the marketing of services is very different. The next chapter is concerned with the application of marketing at the level of the authority as a whole, which is followed in the next chapter by a discussion of the application of marketing ideas to the individual services of the local authority. Local authorities must be concerned not only with marketing their services to the outside world but also with marketing within the organisation itself. Local authorities are highly differentiated organisations involved in a good deal of internal trading and exchange to which a marketing perspective can be applied. These problems are considered in chapter eight. The final chapter contains a discussion of how the marketing perspective might be introduced in local government and argues for a decentralised approach rather than the establishment of marketing departments.

Conclusion

Local authorities are undergoing fundamental change. It is not too difficult to envisage the end of local government, at least in the form that we have know it, and its replacement by a range of special purpose bodies, private sector companies, voluntary agencies, central government control or nothing at all. If it is to survive the threat to its future local government must change. It must become more flexible, faster moving, and more responsive to public needs and wants. Local government has been used to marginal and incremental change; the coming change will not take that form. It will involve fundamental change both in the products and services that the authority provides and in the means of service delivery. The skills of marketing will have a part to play in the design and development of services that are user friendly.

Questions and exercises

▲ *1. What do we mean by the 'public service orientation'? Consider the limitations of the approach of your own authority in the delivery of services to the public and how they might be overcome.*

▲ *2. Is the notion of a public service orientation appropriate in your own service? If not, why not?*

▲ *3. Identify the barriers to responsive public service in your own service.*

▲ *4. Take a particular local authority service. How would you enhance quality, choice, access and participation in that service?*

	Means of enhancement
Quality	
Choice	
Access	
Participation	

▲ *5. Consider a service of the authority that you are familiar with as a user. What do you see as the limitations on quality, choice, access and participation?*

2 Local government is different

Key points

- ▲ *The main arguments that marketing is inappropriate to local government*
- ▲ *Local government is political and marketing and politics do not mix*
- ▲ *Local services should be based on need not market considerations*
- ▲ *Local authorities have limited resources and could not meet the demands that marketing would raise*
- ▲ *Local authorities are not free to respond to the market but must operate within statutory constraint*
- ▲ *Marketing is just another fad*
- ▲ *Local government is about more than consumption*
- ▲ *Each of these arguments is considered and they are argued to be only partially valid*

Local authorities must provide both services and government. They have been the main channels through which the basic services of the welfare state, particularly education, housing and social services, have been delivered. Only the provision of health and social security have been, partly, separate. They are also units of local government, constituted for local choice and for the establishment of local priorities. Local government is a mechanism for the exercise of local choice. A local authority must be concerned with the interdependency between services, for example between housing and social services, or between education and libraries, as well as the provision of individual services. As society has become more complex so these interdependencies have become more important. Local authorities also have a role to play in coping with the major problems and challenges that face British society: urban decay, discrimination against ethnic minority groups, economic and technological change, changing population structures, large-scale unemployment, and a host of others. Local authorities must integrate services to provide effective service to the local community service.

Some would argue that the nature of local government and public service is fundamentally at odds with market processes and marketing approaches. The public service, it may be maintained, is about collective provision for needs rather than the exchange of values. For the socialist or the traditional conservative the market can be seen as an inappropriate mechanism for basic processes of collective provision. The socialist emphasises the equality of rights and the value of products in use, not their exchange value. The paternalist conservative stresses tradition and the role of political obligation and social responsibility. From each of these perspectives the idea of applying marketing techniques in local government can be seen as suspect. The new right, by contrast, argues that the market is the only effective means of distributing goods and ensuring efficient production. The application of market principles within the public service is, at best, a poor substitute for the market itself. Interference with the market, though it might benefit some, will ultimately work to the disbenefit of all by reducing the total amount of goods and services available for distribution. But if one cannot move all the way toward the market then there will still be advantage to be gained from introducing market principles and mechanisms to the public service. Margaret Thatcher and Ronald Reagan have been the leaders of the political arm of this revival of classical economic and social theory, which emphasises the moral value and efficiency of free markets, the minimal state, and individual self-reliance. The intellectual ammunition has been supplied by such thinkers as Hayek and Friedman, and by organisations such as the Adam Smith Institute and the Institute of Economic Affairs.

We cannot discuss the argument over the efficiency of the free market in great detail here, but only in so far as it has relevance for the role of marketing in government. Marketing obviously has a role in the trading organisations that are now being introduced into local government. Direct labour organisations, having to compete for the right to carry out building and highway maintenance work, refuse collection, cleaning and a range of other work, will need marketing skills, if only defensively, to be able to survive and find the work to keep the labour force employed. I believe that the core marketing concepts, of mix, segmentation, and position, can be useful, also, in an approach to local government management that stresses the non-price based allocation of services on the basis of need, for it can aid in the analysis of where need is greatest and what the proper levels of provision are. No technique of social analysis is value-free, and marketing certainly derives from the idea of free markets, but even the most collectivist forms of provision must involve a consideration of, and choice between alternatives. In making choices it is necessary to take account of the needs of the consumers or users of services, and marketing approaches can play a role in this process.

A number of explicit charges can be brought against the use of marketing in the public service:

- Politicians are elected to make decisions and neither can nor should abrogate that responsibility to the market, still less to marketing professionals.
- Public services are provided on the basis of need and should not be subject to exchange in the financial market-place.
- Local government is providing essentially unmarketable services of inspection and control, which people are forced to receive. There is no free market because people cannot choose.
- Local government resources are limited and marketing will simply raise demands and expectations that cannot be met.
- Local authorities are creatures of statute and have no freedom in the goods and services that they deliver.
- Marketing is another managerial fad that will go the way of corporate planning, programming-planning-budgeting-systems and all the rest.
- Local authorities are about more than consumption for they also have a duty to govern. Good government is not a matter that should be marketed.

These objections are serious, and cannot be cast aside lightly. If marketing is to be seen to have any value for local government and other public services then it must respond to these concerns.

The political dimension

Politics is integral to local government, because election provides the legitimacy for control and the exercise of choice by elected members on behalf of the community. The character of local politics has changed radically over the last twenty years: political organisation has become more prevalent, political parties more prominent, and political ideologies more distinct. Manifestos have helped give parties clearer identity, and to be more explicit in what they want the authority to deliver. Parties elected to power in local communities claim a right to implement the manifesto on which they have stood. The British system is one of representative democracy in which politicians, once elected, are free to pursue their own political priorities, within the limits of the law. The reassertion of the political dimension in local government has made the fact that local politics is about local choice clearer.

Marketing may be seen as incompatible with a political perspective. Basic public goods, it may be argued, should not be treated like soap powder, reducing fundamental social choices to the politics of the supermarket. The process of putting one's programme before the public supersedes any notion of marketing. People's lives, it can be maintained, are too important to be left to the dynamics of the marketplace. Politics is about the way that people live, marketing is about what they live with. Political choice can be seen as so fundamental to our lives that it should not be subject to the manipulatory techniques of the marketeer. Local government is a form of representative democracy and the elected representative must make choices on behalf of the local people. Making decision through marketing would be to reduce local government to the politics of the supermarket and would threaten the system of representative democracy. The introduction of marketing approaches will reduce the public domain to being no more than an arena for the pursuit of the politics of the Gross National Appetite.

There are two problems with an argument against the application of marketing techniques based upon the political pre-eminence of the elected councillor and the majority party as the basis of a system of local representative democracy. First, the local mandate is weak. Levels of turnout in local elections average about 40% and in many cases are much less. Further, given the nature of the electoral system, high levels of control of the local council can be gained with relatively low proportions of the vote. The claim that the electorate has voted for the manifesto is also questionable. Few actually see the detailed manifesto, still fewer read it. The claim that the electorate has voted for all the policies in the manifesto is dubious. Finally the results of local elections do not depend only upon local factors, but upon national politics. Miller's study of local voting for the Widdicombe Committee found that relatively few people were strongly swayed by predominantly local factors in the way they cast their votes in local elections. Local factors are important in local elections but they are not the only determinants of their outcome.

For all these reasons, the claim to local political autonomy and the assertion of the purity of representative democracy is weak. People have an interest in local democracy that goes beyond the casting of a generalised vote. There is a need to develop participative as well a representative democracy. People are concerned to have some input into those services that have a direct impact upon them. there are a number of forms of participation that are possible, and different approaches will be necessary in different circumstances. We can consider that nature of participation as a ladder. At the bottom is manipulation and at the top direct citizen control. Arnstein presents the ladder as follows:

Arnstein's Ladder of Participation
Citizen control
Delegated power
Partnership
Placation
Consultation
Informing
Therapy
Manipulation

We will argue later that the more a service involves the user then the more important it is to develop higher levels of participation. Generally representative democracy needs to be supplemented by other methods of citizen involvement if it is to be accepted as legitimate and accountable. People will become suspicious of services that they cannot influence and will cease to value them.

The need to adopt a marketing approach, focusing upon the needs that people have and the benefits that they receive from services, is an addition to, not a substitute for, representative democracy. The marketing focus on exchange is not an argument for exchange in a financial market, but for thinking through what it is that is being exchanged in each service encounter. Local government is not simply a system for providing people with a series of free gifts, but also makes demands for them, for obedience, support or commitment. Citizens have duties as well as rights. The marketing focus can help us to be clear about these demands and the nature of the transactions involved in giving and receiving support, as well as the benefits that people receive from local authorities.

In a more mundane way, marketing techniques might be used to analyse why voting turnouts are so low in many local elections. It would be valuable to know more about who did and who did not vote, and why people behaved as they did. This sort of research would be no different from the market research that is done to determine why people do and do not use products. It would also be useful to know what costs and benefits people saw in voting. Promotion campaigns might well be used to improve turnout. There is a tendency to accept the low turnout in local elections as a fact of nature. It is not. It is susceptible to change, if we understand why it is as low as it is. It is difficult to argue that research and promotion related to local elections would damage local democracy. Marketing can contribute to, as much as undermine, the political nature of the local authority as long as those applying marketing concepts and thinking are clear on the nature of the political context. Certainly marketing cannot replace the need for political decision.

Need and use

Clearly local authorities are established to provide goods and services that people need and that have value in use, rather than simply exchange value on the market. The basis of the welfare state is that people have a right to have at least basic needs met, within the limits of social and economic capacity. There is inevitably an element of redistribution from the more to the less advantaged in the provision of state services. It could not be otherwise in a humane society. The values of equality, at least of opportunity, and fairness, underpin the provision of public services. Marketing, seen as how to sell goods to those who can pay for them, can be argued to be incompatible with the social philosophy of welfare. This is a serious argument because the local authority is not simply about the delivery of individual services but also works to express a particular political and social philosophy in its actions. The adoption of a marketing approach, it might be argued, would undermine the value base of the local authority.

A simple radical response to this argument might be that the whole basis of the welfare state is wrong, the world simply is not fair, and equality is not attainable, desirable or efficient. Interference with free market mechanisms will simply result in everybody being worse off than they would otherwise have been. The sooner we make the market the basis of as much local provision as possible the better. This is the argument that is made by such thinkers as Milton Friedman and Friedrich von Hayek. Some, such as Milton Friedman's son David, go further and argue for anarcho-capitalism, the more or less complete replacement of the state with free markets. More or less everything including law and order, the production of money, the judicial system and even defence would be provided through free market mechanisms. Few would accept the full blooded case for markets, but the role of markets in signalling wants and distributing goods and services efficiently is now being more widely accepted. Even in an essentially non-market system, market mechanisms can play a valuable role in providing information on which to base the provision of service.

Administration and voting are not enough to signal the nature of people's needs nor do they provide any very clear picture of what it is that people want. Though needs cannot be equated with wants there is an element of want involved in the definition of need. The danger of a purely political and administrative approach is that the politicians' and administrators' views of need replace those of people themselves. In a culturally complex society other signals are needed as well as the vote. Even if notions of equality and fairness are to underlie the distribution of certain goods and services, market research approaches can be used to determine what peoples' needs are. We cannot assume that professionals necessarily know what is good for people never mind what they think their needs are. The development of markets within the public sector may also aid more efficient distribution. Even in a system based on need and use, markets and marketing can have a function in targeting provision, through telling us where needs are greatest.

There is extensive evidence that the relatively advantaged middle-classes have gained more from the welfare state than the relatively disadvantaged, because they have been able to understand and manipulate the system better. Much of the failure of services arises because people are unaware of their existence or do not know how to use them. Marketing techniques of analysis may help to determine more clearly who needs to benefit from services, and how to distribute them effectively. Mimicking market mechanisms, by, for example, distributing vouchers, may help old people to get their needs met more precisely, and to obtain the appropriate package of services. It is not markets or marketing that are incompatible with distribution based upon need, but the ability to buy being based on criteria that have nothing to do with social circumstances.

Control and surveillance

Marketing can be seen as inappropriate for some of the services that local authorities must deliver. A local authority must deliver 'public goods'. That is goods which it is not possible to stop people from receiving benefit, even if they do not pay, and where any use of the good by one person does not prevent use by another. Clean air or a pleasant environment are examples of such goods. The fact that I enjoy an unpolluted environment does not stop anyone else from doing so, and we cannot exclude people from the benefits of a cleaner environment. Certainly marketing will not be applicable to such goods in the same way as it is to soap powder or to motor cars, but the principles may still be useful in two ways. First, marketing techniques can help make clear the choices that are available, for example between pollution and economic development. There are well developed marketing techniques for trading off the various characteristics of goods that may conflict with each other that could be used in the analysis of public goods. Second, promotion will often play a large part in the development and maintenance of public attitudes and values towards public goods. Advertising and promotion, for example, might be used to produce attitudes that are favourable towards less pollution of the environment. Indeed, I shall argue later that marketing can have a strong role to play in making more apparent the benefits from public goods. The problem of such goods is often that their intangibility makes them easy to ignore and hard to judge.

Marketing may also seem inappropriate for control and inspection services. Local authorities are heavily involved in such services, for example building control, food inspection and licensing. Social services have a control function in relation to children and the mentally ill, and must inspect private sector residential homes. The fire service inspects and licenses buildings. The police are obviously heavily involved in various forms of control. In all of these cases, and in other aspects of control, it can be argued that the local authority is enforcing the law, rather than providing a service. Marketing might simply allow people to say that they did not want to use these onerous services.

Again it can be argued that the problem is not whether or not a marketing focus applies, but how it might be used given the nature of the service. In the case of inspection and control services the problem is one of being clear about who the client or the customer is, which will not always be easy to determine. In the case of food inspection it is not so much those who sell food as those who buy it. In social services there are moral dilemmas in defining who the client is and distinguishing between the rights of children, parents and families. Again the marketing role will be limited but benefit analysis, segmentation and promotion are ideas that might prove valuable in identifying the customer and ensuring that these services reach those for whom they are intended. The difficulty with many control services is to identify the beneficiaries. In some cases the beneficiary may be the community as a whole.

Promotion may be important for these services. In some cases they are subject to competition. Building control services must now compete with the private sector and the national representatives of building control professionals have launched a promotion campaign. Indeed it is the anonymity of some services such as trading standards and environmental protection, and their popular identification with weights and measures and rat-catching, which limit their effectiveness. Services are likely to be less effective if the public has little knowledge about them. It is precisely because of their generalised nature that control services need to think carefully about who their consumers and customers are and how the profile of the service can be raised.

Resource limitation

A common claim, when the question of getting closer to the public is raised, is to argue that this will simply encourage a demand that cannot be satisfied. There is little point in raising expectations that cannot be satisfied. If we ask people to notify us of potholes in the road or of street lamps that are not working or of their needs for housing or housing repairs then we will simply have a better knowledge of the demand that we cannot meet. The real problem is that there are inadequate resources in the face of great need. If one raises expectations one will simply place a greater load on those who might tell the consumers what they cannot have. On this argument more resources would make marketing irrelevant.

This view assumes that marketing is about maximising sales, but that is not so. Nor is it the case that a marketing perspective has nothing to say in the face of shortage, whether relative or absolute. First, it may be useful to consider the analogy between limited resources and the marketing of absolutely limited goods. Many goods are absolutely limited at any given time. If seats on an aeroplane or in a theatre, or rooms in a hotel are not sold they cannot be stored for future use. But, equally those marketing these services will not want to have over-full demand, which will take up staff time to no great purpose. These problems do not make marketing irrelevant, but require specific approaches to segmentation, promotion and sales. Sophisticated queuing and booking techniques have been developed in some cases, often using new technology, as in the case of airlines. In some cases demarketing, as Kotler calls it, has been developed, that is the systematic discouragement of excess demand. The point is not to prevent use but to target provision. A clear market analysis will consider how a limited product can best be distributed.

A second approach to absolutely limited services is remarketing, which involves not simply discouraging demand but also encouraging other patterns of demand or behaviour. This approach may be particularly useful for the promotion of social behaviour or ideas. Care in the community, for example, is an attempt at remarketing in the sense of trying to develop alternative social expectations and behaviour where we do not expect the old or people with disabilities simply to disappear into residential care. The point is that one does not want to create maximum demand and then not meet it. But the information that may be generated by a marketing approach can be used to match supply to demand. Resource constraints will always be a major concern for the local authority, and for other public services such as the National Health Service. Potential demand is likely to continue to be greater than the resources available. This does not mean that a marketing perspective is invalid, but rather that the marketing approach adopted will be different from cases in which the intention is to maximise demand. At the least, reliable and valid market information will be needed to be able to plan how services are to be delivered. Resource constraint also means giving clear attention to the income side, and therefore to pricing policy which is an aspect of the marketing management function.

The constraints of statute

Local authorities are creatures of statute. They operate under an *ultra vires* rule whereby they may not do anything that they have not been specifically empowered to do. They have only very limited general powers to spend on activities which are considered to be for the good of the community, as opposed to statutory services. It may be argued that authorities cannot, therefore, make their own decisions on products and markets and so the whole concept of marketing is irrelevant. This might be especially so when faced with central government, which has been tightening up on discretion over the last ten years and which has become more concerned with national standards. Developments such as the national curriculum in education might be seen as limiting even further the autonomy of the local authority.

The theory of statutory constraint is much stronger than the practice. Certainly local authorities' basic powers and duties are laid down in statute but in practice there are a whole range of creative ways that can be found to develop services. The creative imagination of local government has been illustrated and, perhaps, wasted by the whole range of financial devices known as creative accountancy. But various approaches to funding and joint co-operation with other agencies, as well as grant aiding have been used to develop services, for example in housing or social services. Nor are the statutory constraints themselves tightly drawn. Authorities are required to carry out certain functions and to deliver certain services, but little is normally specified about the level of service, the precise form it shall take, how quickly it shall be provided, or who are to be the precise recipients of the service. Even where national standards exist, for example on physical school space per pupil, or response times for the fire service, there is still wide variation in the actual nature of provision. The means by which services should be provided are rarely specified. Local authorities normally choose to do so by the employment of their own labour, to provide the service directly, but there is no requirement for them to do so. A whole range of alternative means are possible using the voluntary sector, contracting out of services, agencies with other authorities, shared facilities, partnerships with the private sector and a host of other approaches.

So wide are the possibilities that it is possible to maintain that the *ultra vires* rule plays little part in local decisions. If local authorities want to do something, they will usually be able to find a way. It is only at the extreme that things are closed off by statute, and even then there will be room for variation between authorities. Marketing is not made irrelevant by statutory constraint because there is a great deal of choice available within the statutory framework. Marketing techniques may contribute to the way that choice is made.

Marketing— a new fad?

Maybe the marketing perspective, and the public service orientation to which it contributes, is just a new fad. Like other passing enthusiasms, such as skateboards, hula hoops and corporate planning, it will fade. This cynical view is at variance with the way that organisations tend to develop. They do not normally pick up new approaches, run them for a while and then drop them, returning to the old ways. There may be broad cycles, for example of authoritarian and participative management, reflecting long-term fluctuations in the economy, but most approaches get adopted, modified and routinised into the organisation. Scientific management, human relations and marketing itself, in the private sector, have all gone through this process. Corporate planning provides an example for local government. Since the 1970s, when it first came into local authorities, it has become part of the normal routine in many authorities. The name has been abandoned in many cases, and over-elaborate approaches have been toned down, but much of the approach persists, and has become part of the normal organisational routine.

Marketing is likely to go through the same process because it is dealing with fundamental aspects of the services that local authorities provide. The perceived need for a new approach to local authority management is both wide and deep and marketing is likely to play a major part. It is not simply a fad, but a realisation of a deep problem in the nature of public service. The need for good service relationships with the customer has been realised in many private sector companies, especially in service organisations. In the public service it is more important, not less, that a better relationship is developed with those who use services because the services provided are more fundamental to people's lives.

Consumers or customers

The problems in applying the concepts of marketing in the local authority context are reflected in the difficulty of knowing what language to use. Marketing theories and ideas cannot be straightforwardly applied in the local government context because the product and the relationship with the user are different from the case of the market. The notion of consumers or customers clearly does not capture the essence of the relationship between the citizen and the local authority. Stacey says, in the slightly different context of the National Health Service:

> . . . The concept of the patient as consumer undervalues the patient status. In the ideal of free, perfect competition, the consumer held high status; the consumer was always right. In monopoly capitalism, in the high bureaucracies of the welfare state, this is no longer true. In these circumstances the consumer has low status. What else are all the consumers' rights movements about? Only the disadvantaged or threatened develop movements to enhance or defend their rights.

Certainly, as Stacey argues, the concept of consumer does not capture the way that the patient is both a co-worker and a work-object. The position of the recipients of education or social services are similar. The notion of consumer is inadequate because it implies a largely passive approach — others produce the service, I simply consume it, and the only influence that I have is whether I consume it or not, and, perhaps, not even that.

Customer is an even less appropriate word for the public sector. It is the crucial word for the private sector, as Peters and Waterman have emphasised with their concept of 'closeness to the customer'. 'Customer' carries connotations of economic exchange that are inappropriate in caring services and in many public services generally. It also implies a directness of relationship that may be inadequate to describe collectively provided public goods or control and protective services. Finally, 'customer' hardly captures the position where people are forced to receive service, and have little choice over where, when and how they receive it, as with some aspects of education. In some cases 'customer' may be an apt description; for example in the case of leisure services or lending libraries, but for most it will not be adequate.

Other words are available to describe these to whom local authorities provide services. We might talk of:

▽ Clients
▽ Users
▽ Recipients
▽ Beneficiaries

as well as customers.

'Client' is equally inappropriate as a universal description of those who use local authority services. The word client has been used by social services in imitation of lawyers and other professionals. It carries connotations of individual, personal service that would not carry over into other services. It hardly seems to make sense to talk of the clients of the police or the fire services still less of the highways department. The word client also have notions of freedom of use that fit ill even with some cases in the social services, for example care orders.

'User' carries many of the same connotations of passivity as does consumer. It also bears a utilitarian sense that does not encompass notions of need nor take account of the responsibilities as well as the rights of the user. 'Beneficiary' is a useful concept for collectively provided goods, where there is no individual consumer. Benefit analysis helps us to be clear about who benefits from the service. But, again, it is very passive in its connotations. 'Recipient' also has passive connotations and implies that there is a clearly identifiable individual who receives the service, which may not be the case, for example for public goods that are collectively consumed.

Each of the various words available to describe those who receive local authority services have both valuable and confusing aspects. This is especially so when the person who directly consumes the service is not the only beneficiary, as when parents, employers or the whole community gain benefit from childrens' education, or where client and user are separate, for example when social services help those caring for people with a mental handicap. Some of the words are more useful in some services than others.

Different words will be appropriate in different circumstances and in different services. It is necessary to have more than one word to describe the relationship between the local authority and those who receive because the relationship is itself multidimensional. The table below gives some examples of the words that

People's relationship to services

	Consumer	Customer	User	Client	Beneficiary	Recipient
Social Services						
Education						
Transport						
Police						
Fire						
Leisure						
Housing						
Roads						
Environmental health						
Trading standards						
Street lighting						
Refuse collection						
Adult education						
Libraries						
Old people's homes						

might be appropriate for some general service areas and some specific services. The table might be filled out by marking which description of the people for whom the service is provided are most appropriate. For refuse collection has customers, for example for trade refuse, and people generally benefit from having the refuse dealt with effectively. Social services has clients, though other words may be more appropriate to certain aspects of the service.

In fact, the analysis of the relationship between services and those they are provided for is part of the market segmentation and positioning process, which will be discussed in the next chapter. Deciding whether a particular person or group are users, beneficiaries, or whatever, partly depends upon the position that the authority wants to adopt towards them. It is not only that the different words involve different concepts of the relationship with those to whom services are delivered, but that they involve choices between alternative approaches to the delivery of service.

There are three ways of dealing with the problem of the appropriate description of the complex nature of the relationship involved in public service use. First we could abandon the attempt, and simply say that silly questions are being raised. I take it that this is an inadequate response to what are real questions. The second is to invent a new word or acronym that captures the complexities such as Toffler's 'prosumer' to capture the fact that the consumer is co-producer in service industries. I do not think this is adequate, not least because part of the problem is that different relations and characteristics apply in different cases. I shall adopt the third, pragmatic, solution of using the whole range of words depending on the context. I shall also use the word 'consumer' to talk about the general relationship of people to local authorities, even though it has some connotations that are misleading.

The debate over the proper description of those who receive public services reflects a set of genuine problems. The professional domination of local government, with professionals deciding what is best for people, is coming to be questioned. Local authorities are trying to establish a new relationship with the communities they serve. There is a need to be clearer about the services that are being provided. Large public bureaucracies must reconsider the way that they are organised and face competition from other organisations. The debate is not one of semantics, but reflects deep ambiguities in the nature of local services.

A marketing approach

It would be foolish to argue that marketing was either a panacea or that the approach could simply be taken over from the private sector and grafted onto the local authority. Different circumstances demand different approaches, both in terms of content and in the ways that the function is structured into the organisation. Local authorities are not like private sector companies, and they have responsibilities that private companies do not. Some of the services of the local authority, such as tourism, will be very amenable to commercial styles of marketing. In other cases, the police or social services, it will be much more difficult.

Marketing is a mixture of perspective, process and techniques. In some parts of the local authority it will be possible to use all three. In others the perspective may apply, but the various techniques available will be much less relevant. The differences between the local authority and other types of organisations do not mean that marketing techniques are not applicable but that we must be clear on the differences if they are to have relevance.

Questions and Exercises

▲ *1. List the arguments for and against the use of marketing in local government*
▲ *2. Which of these arguments do you think are the strongest?*
▲ *3. Marketing concepts are obviously more appropriate for some services than others. Which services do you feel are most amenable to the use of marketing?*
▲ *4. Consider the various words used to describe those to whom you provide service. Consider whether they are best described as:*

Customers
Users
Clients
Consumers
Beneficiaries

▲ *5. What other words can be used to describe those who use your service? Do they adequately capture the nature of the service relationship?*

Part II
The nature of marketing

3 What is marketing?

Key points

- ▲ *Marketing as part of the general function of management.*
- ▲ *The two main aspects of marketing — strategic marketing and consumer marketing.*
- ▲ *The strategic marketing process: determining the broad market area of operation, market research, market segmentation and positioning, and the marketing mix.*
- ▲ *Analysing the market area — portfolio methods of analysis.*
- ▲ *The stages of the research process and approaches to market research. Market research is just research.*
- ▲ *Segmenting the market, the importance of benefit, group and situation of use.*
- ▲ *Market position, targeting or saturation approaches.*
- ▲ *The components of the marketing mix, product, price, promotion and place.*

Marketing is concerned with the process of relations with the consumer, and has an effect on every aspect of the organisation from product research and design to after-sales support. One of the reasons that people with a marketing background have achieved dominant positions in modern companies is the breadth of their links and interests. Marketing, as a management process, is partly technique and partly philosophy. Like all professionals marketers tend to claim that their expertise derives partly from rigorous technical knowledge and partly from more nebulous qualities and attitudes that can only be acquired through experience. Both technique and experience are necessary, though the balance will vary with the context. Neither the techniques nor the expertise are the sole preserve of the marketing experts. Knowledge of statistical research techniques, or questionnaire design for market research may be widely spread within the local authority. Many employees will also have practical experience of marketing though they may not have called it that. The activities of a manager may have been concerned with promotion, public relations, product design, or research, all of which have strong links with marketing. Marketing is part of the general management role.

There are two fundamental aspects of marketing:

- ▽ Strategic analysis
- ▽ Consumer analysis

Strategic analysis is concerned with determining how the values and purposes of the organisation can be achieved. It is the process by which organisation resources are mobilised, within the constraints that are faced. The development of strategy has both an internal focus, upon the strengths and weaknesses of the organisation, and an external focus upon the world in which it must live, with the threats that the external context poses and the opportunities it creates. Strategy also includes a notion of time and of scope. It is concerned with the medium and the long term rather than the immediate, and with broad directions rather than detail. Strategic analysis is concerned with which products we will produce for which markets, and how we will distribute them. Finally strategy is concerned with how others, both consumers and producers will react to what the organisation does. We are always operating in a world in which the outcomes of our actions depend upon the way that others act and how they react to what we do.

Consumer analysis is concerned with understanding how those who receive goods and services experience them. There is a great deal of work on how consumers make decisions about buying goods, much less on other aspects of the consumption process. We need to know much more about the determinants of satisfaction and what quality means to consumers. British Airways, in its attempt to develop more customer conscious service, found, through research, that four things were expected by customers.

- ▽ Care and concern by contact people.
- ▽ Problem-solving capacity in front line personnel.
- ▽ Spontaneity and flexibility in the application of policies and procedures.
- ▽ Recover, the ability of front line people to put things right when they have gone wrong.

Only the first and third of these had been considered by British Airways; the importance of the others had never been realised. What is important to the consumer will be different for different products and in different organisations. There has been relatively little study of the process of consumption in the service sector.

I shall discuss the consumption process in the following chapter; in this chapter I shall concern myself with the strategic aspects of marketing.

Strategic marketing

Those familiar with corporate planning will recognise much of strategic marketing as being old ideas with a face lift. Strategic market planning and corporate management are close cousins. The difference, perhaps, is a clearer focus on the outside world rather than the internal aspects of the organisation. The strategic marketing approach has the following stages:

Determine broad market area
↓
Market analysis and research
↓
Market segmentation
↓
Market positioning
↓
Market mix

The authority must make decisions in each of these five areas if it is to be able to produce services designed for specific sections of the market.

Market area

The decision about which broad markets to be in is crucial for any organisation. No organisation wants to be trapped in a declining market, or to produce products for a market that never comes into being. A number of models have been developed for examining the possibilities of different markets — for determining the organisation's portfolio of products. The best known are those of the Boston Consulting Group and the General Electric Company, both of which provide methods of analysing the portfolio of products that are or could be provided. The Boston Consulting Group base their analysis around the concept of market share and market growth, which can both be divided into high and low, giving the following pattern.

Market share	Market Growth: High	Market Growth: Low
High	Stars	Cash cows
Low	Prospects	Dogs

Figure 3.1. Boston Consulting Group matrix
Source: Johnson, G., Scholes, K. *Exploring Corporate Strategy*

The most attractive products are the stars, which have high growth potential and for which the organisations share of the market is high. Investment is justified to ensure market dominance and will yield high profits. Star products will be at the centre of an organisations marketing strategy. 'Cash cows', by contrast, have a limited long-term future and warrant little investment, but may be used as a source of funds to release capital for more lucrative long-term investments in other products. 'Prospects' are products where investment might be justified, but is more speculative, and 'dogs' are products that should be discontinued, because they provide neither cash nor prospects. Companies will have a mixture of products and the point is to ensure that 'dogs' are discontinued as soon as possible, and 'prospects' converted into stars.

Another method of portfolio analysis has been developed by McKinsey and General Electric based upon competitive position and market attractiveness. An organisation might have a strong competitive position, based upon cost advantages, or a strong product. Large growing markets are likely to be attractive. The matrix illustrated in figure 3.2 can then be developed. Organisations will obviously want to be in markets that are highly attractive and in which they have a strong competitive position.

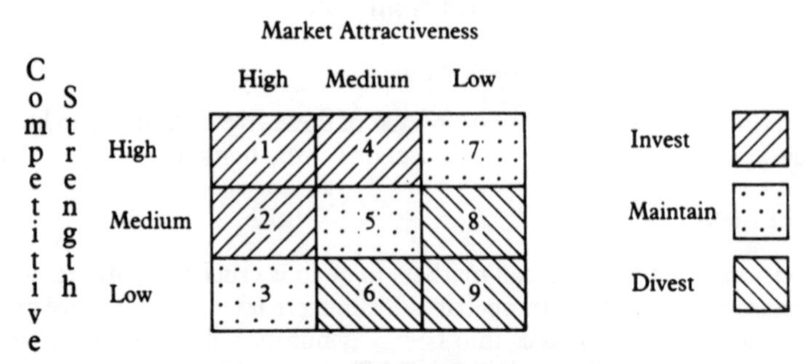

Figure 3.2. General Electric matrix
Source: Johnson, G., Scholes, K.

The organisation should invest in the three north-west quadrants (1,2,4), maintain its position in the three quadrants along the south-west/north-east diagonal (3,5,7) and move out of, or milk, products in the three south-east quadrants (6,8,9).

Matrices such as these can be built up using a range of indicators of the key dimensions of organisation and market. Statistical techniques can be used to develop multi-dimensional analysis of products, but in most cases, simple two-dimensional analysis will be enough. The indicators to be used in the portfolio analysis will depend upon the particular organisation and context. In the private sector the concern will be with how products in the portfolio contribute to profit; companies will want a portfolio of strong products that contribute to profits, and that have a strong potential for growth. In the public sector the concern will not be with profit and growth but with other objectives such as the degree of need or the extensiveness of social problems. But all organisations, given scarce resources, will need to trade off investments between the products or services that they produce. A local authority, for example, might analyse services in terms of need and the level of provision by other organisations, yielding the following matrix:

Provision By Other Agencies		Need: High	Need: Low
	High	Targeted Provision	No Provision
	Low	Extensive Provision	Encourage provision by other agencies

Figure 3.3. Need and provision matrix

The authority might then play a strong role in cases of high need, either by itself providing on an extensive or universal scale where there are few or no other providers, or targeting on those who are neglected by other providers. Where there is low need, but no alternative sources of provision, the authority might play a networking and stimulating role. The authority might play no role where there is low need but many other providers. Local authority housing provides an example of targeted provision, education of extensive provision and areas of social services of encouraging other agencies. Examples of no provision are services from which local authorities might withdraw such as providing washing facilities. Individual services could examine the portfolio of services that they provide, for example the make-up of social services or police services.

Other factors might be considered in creating a product analysis matrix in the local authority:

▽ Expertise
▽ Statutory duty
▽ Availability of finance
▽ Political pressure

- ∇ Public expectation
- ∇ Required if other services are to be effective
- ∇ Government pressure
- ∇ Professional preference

Each authority will need to determine what are, for it, the important factors in determining the service portfolio that it should develop.

The next step is to use the portfolio analysis to decide on the strategy for service development. Again, this depends on the relationship between products and markets. When faced with threats organisations may choose either to defend their existing product positions or be innovative. The distinction can be illustrated by a third matrix, illustrated in figure 3.4, using the two dimensions of new and existing markets and new and existing products.

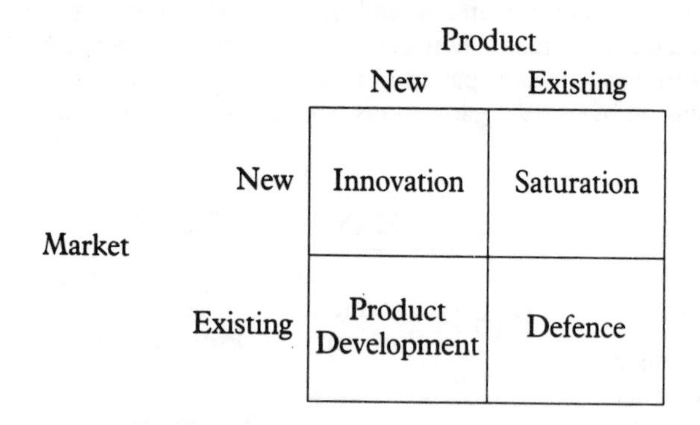

Figure 3.4. Market development strategy

Organisations may adopt a purely defensive strategy of staying with existing products in existing markets and simply trying to sell more of them, perhaps only to existing customers. This strategy may be relatively effective, at least in the short term, if the customer can be tied to the producer, for example through rental agreements for equipment. But such a strategy is dangerous and is unlikely to work in the long term, particularly if the market is likely to decline. A market saturation strategy involves trying to sell existing products in new markets. It is, in a sense, selling what you can make rather than making what you can sell. Organisations may develop new products for existing markets — product development — or adopt a total innovation strategy of developing new products for new markets. Local authorities exhibit examples of each of these strategies. The defensive strategy is, perhaps, the most common as local authorities try to maintain services in the face of declining demand or finance. But local authorities have had to search for new markets for existing products, for example in the case of direct labour organisations faced with increased competition or declining work, and for new products for existing markets, for example in education or libraries. Local authorities may also be innovative, developing wholly new services such as tourism, or the development of products, such as uPVC windows, for sale.

These types of analysis allow organisations to decide what sort of product market they want to be in and whether they want to change or stay as they are. The decisions involve a combination of weighing the nature of the organisation, the market and the environment. The organisation must determine the key dimensions for analysis of its market, and then determine how they relate to each other.

Market analysis and research

Detailed market information is necessary if the organisation is to be able to make specific decisions and monitor their impact. Information will normally be available from a number of sources. The organisation will have its own internal records. The development of new technology has allowed organisations to make far more flexible use of their records. Much information is also available from published sources, such as government reports and statistics. Again the development of new technology has expanded the availability of information giving organisations access to a large number of data banks. Market research studies may need to be commissioned from commercial market researchers for specific purposes. Larger organisations may have their own market research capacity, but most will use specialist market research companies for more sophisticated studies. Local authorities and central government are increasingly using market research organisations such as MORI and Gallup to gather data.

Market research may cover a wide range of topics. Research on what consumers buy and how they explain why they behave the way they do has been extensive. It is heavily based in individual psychology and is reviewed in the next chapter. Other areas of research include (Cowell 1984):

▽ research on markets
▽ research on products
▽ research on promotion
▽ research on distribution
▽ research on pricing

Indeed market research pervades the whole process from product design to delivery. More research at the design stage will often save a great deal of work later on and it is fair to say that more research will be necessary on the design of services in local government in future as the world becomes more complex and services need to become more sophisticated in response.

Market research

The need for market research may arise at any stage in the marketing process, from analysing the various segments in the market to understanding the competition, from designing the services to assessing the effectiveness of different promotion techniques. A number of local authorities have now begun to use market research, particularly in surveying public satisfaction with services. Market research can be an expensive process if it involves using specialist market research firms, but local authorities should be able to do most of the research that they need themselves. Highly sophisticated research will only be necessary in cases where the authority must make major decisions and has little information.

The research process

The market research process has a number of stages:

- ∇ Identification of the research problem
- ∇ Determination of the type of research needed.
- ∇ Determination of information needs.
- ∇ Decide on methods of data gathering.
- ∇ Design research
- ∇ Gather data.
- ∇ Analyse data.
- ∇ Presentation of results.

I shall consider each of these in turn.

IDENTIFYING THE PROBLEM

The key to good market research is a clear definition of the research problem. This is a job for the service manager and not for the market research specialist. Managers need to be clear on why they want the research and what it is to be used for. They must also be clear on who is to use it and how they will do so. It is important to be as specific as possible on what the problem is because otherwise it will not be clear how the research can help management. General questions cannot produce specific answers. It is better to ask:

> What should be the opening hours of X branch library if it is to be used best by people between the ages of 60 and 75?

than:

> How many hours a week should libraries open if old people are to use them?

Only those who manage the service can know the questions that need to be asked, though marketing experts might help them to formulate the problem clearly. The formulation of the research question will be the result of a process of dialogue between the researcher and the manager who wants to know the answer.

DETERMINATION OF THE TYPE OF RESEARCH

The more complex the problem the more difficult the research is likely to be. We may distinguish three types of market research:

- ∇ Factual: to determine basic factual information, such as times of use of services, such as bus services or libraries. A factual question would be: 'How many people used the number 10 bus, on average, on Monday morning over the last month between 7 am and 9 am?'
- ∇ Attitudinal: To determine the subjective views that people hold for example whether they are satisfied with a service or not. An attitudinal question would be: 'How satisfied are those who use them with the play facilities in X park?'
- ∇ Causal: to determine relationships, for example whether more street lighting will reduce levels of crime, or why children fail to attend school. A causal question would be: 'Why do housing tenants on X estate fall into rent arrears more than other similar estates?'

It will be relatively straightforward to discover factual matters, such as when people use public transport or patterns of library usage. Attitudes are more difficult to discover, and to determine causal relationships more difficult still. For example, it may be extremely difficult to discover why people do or do not use a particular service, partly because they themselves may have very little idea. The more difficult the research the more expensive it will be, and the less likely it is that the organisation or department will be able to do it itself. It will also take a great deal longer to answer complicated than straightforward questions. Given the cost and difficulty of research it is important that the organisation is sure that it wants and needs the information before setting out on the research process.

INFORMATION NEEDS

Having determined what sort of problems we are dealing with, and what sort of research will provide the answer, we can examine information needs. In many cases we will not need original research and can rely upon available information – secondary sources. We might, for example, get the necessary information from:

- ▽ Previously published studies
- ▽ Information the authority already possesses
- ▽ National government departments
- ▽ Academic institutions
- ▽ Libraries
- ▽ Specialist information services, such as the Education Management Information Service (EMIS) or the Local Authorities Race Relations Information Exchange (LARRIE).
- ▽ Research done by other authorities.

Secondary data has the advantage of being cheap and readily available. It has also, very often, been collected and presented in a way that may be much more readily intelligible than complex original studies.

Primary data, information collected specifically for the research study being considered, should only be gathered when all secondary sources have been exhausted. The first part of any market research study is a review of the existing secondary sources. The more one is dependent upon primary sources the longer and the more expensive the research process will be. In evaluating the need for primary research local authorities need to compare the cost of gathering the information with the benefit that will be obtained from it.

RESEARCH DESIGN

If it is decided that primary information is necessary and that it is worth gathering, then we will need to design the research project. This will involve:

- ▽ Determining the various stages of the research
- ▽ Determining the method of study
- ▽ Developing a detailed research timetable.

The research design and timetable will need to flow from the general to the particular. The review of information and studies already available will provide guidance, for example, for unstructured interviews, which may be used as the basis for detailed surveys.

GATHER DATA

Only after going through all of the previous stages should we actually start collecting information. There are a number of means of gathering data:

- ▽ Observation – for example counting how many people use an office over a given period, or observing how people behave.
- ▽ Interviews, which may be structured, following a specific list of questions, or unstructured, exploring topics in a more flexible way.
- ▽ Group discussions, which may be very valuable for exploring ill-understood issues.
- ▽ Postal surveys.
- ▽ Telephone surveys.
- ▽ Panels of people, regularly surveyed to assess changes over time.
- ▽ Gathering statistical data from government sources and other data archives.

Observation is fairly straightforward, and is most useful for simple questions, where objective information is readily available. Unstructured and semi-structured interviews are appropriate particularly for exploratory research and for detailed understanding of attitudes. Panels are useful for monitoring a service over time and for building a continuous process of research into service planning. A number of authorities are now operating panels of this sort, for example in monitoring leisure use. Group discussions are relatively cheap, and, if well-structured and organised, can provide a great deal of information, for example in the early stages of service design. They are widely used in product development and product design.

Surveys are now being widely used in local government, most commonly to assess satisfaction with services. Most surveys will involve sampling, that is selecting a number of people from the population group that is being researched. Only in very small populations will a total survey be possible. There are a number of types of sample:

- ▽ Probability sample, in which each individual in the population has a known chance of being selected.
- ▽ Random sample, where each individual has an equal chance of being selected.
- ▽ Stratified sampling: dividing the population into groups and sampling from each group, for example sampling from different age groups, or from different socio-economic groupings.
- ▽ Quota sampling: requiring a given number of individuals with specific characteristics to be surveyed, for example requiring a given number of women or single parents.

The size of the sample depends upon

- ▽ How confident you want to be that the results you get are characteristics of the population and not just of the sample.
- ▽ How accurate you want your results to be.

Larger samples are required for higher levels of accuracy and confidence. The size of sample that you need is not dependent upon the size of the population that you are studying. Big populations do not require huge samples to be taken if they are to be understood properly. Samples in the range 300 to 500 would normally be adequate for most purposes. Increasing the size of the survey sample will increase the confidence and accuracy of the results much more slowly, so that buying a more accurate result can lead to rapidly escalating costs. Managers will need to provide guidance to those doing the research on the confidence in and accuracy of the results that they want. The researcher will then be able to apply the appropriate statistical procedures. The accuracy that is required will depend upon how likely it is that a mistake will be made and how much impact such a mistake would have.

There will inevitably be non-respondents in surveys. In postal surveys responses of 30–50% should be possible and in telephone surveys 60–80%. Response to postal surveys can be increased by:

- ▽ Enclosing pre-paid envelopes for return.
- ▽ Writing good covering letters.
- ▽ Making clear the purpose of the research and how it will be used.
- ▽ Not asking sensitive questions if they are not necessary.
- ▽ Designing the survey well.
- ▽ Careful ordering of the questions, for example not starting straight off with the most sensitive matters.
- ▽ Good presentation of material.
- ▽ Reminders and follow-ups.
- ▽ Promising to feed back the results if relevant.

The cost of conducting surveys can be reduced if the authority is willing to do some of the work, for example by posting questionnaires, doing an initial design of the questionnaire or doing some of the sampling. One should work to increase the response rate rather than the size of the sample if a larger number of responses is wanted. It will generally be better to have a large response from a smaller sample than a very low response from a larger sample.

Questionnaires are difficult to design. A number of features need to be considered.

- ▽ Length: the longer a questionnaire is the less likely it is to be completed.
- ▽ Complexity: the more difficult it is to complete the lower the response will be.
- ▽ The nature of the individual questions: questions should be simple and clear, and the responses easy to interpret. It is important that questions only call for one response, and one should not ask such questions as 'Is the service quick and efficient?' when the response might refer either to 'quick' or 'efficient'.
- ▽ The type of response: questions may invite either open-ended responses or a fixed choice between specified responses.
- ▽ The order of questions: normally one will proceed from the general to the particular.

The less time it takes to complete a questionnaire the better, and once the time taken gets beyond 15–20 minutes there will be a rapid falling away of response. Before any questionnaire is used it will need to be pilot-tested, to ensure that it can be completed and produces sensible results, and revised in the light of the test.

ANALYSIS AND PRESENTATION

Extremely sophisticated techniques have been developed for analysing market research data but, in most cases, local authorities will only need relatively simple statistical techniques. The availability of computers has made it possible to process large amounts of data, and to submit it to various tests. The important thing is that the data should be analysed and presented in a way that can be understood by those who are to use it. Much of the failing of research lies in the presentation. There is little purpose in brilliant and illuminating research if it cannot be understood by the potential user or does not get to the people who need to know about it. As much attention needs to be given to dissemination and the use of research as it is to actually carrying it out.

RESEARCH AND EXPERIMENTATION

Most market research will involve gathering data of the sort considered above but other approaches are possible. A service may be market tested on an experimental basis, for example we might vary office opening hours, put buses on new routes, try out new methods of teaching or test new road surfacing materials. Experimentation may be difficult when people may feel discriminated against, or in highly sensitive services such as social services, but it is a powerful means of assessing acceptability and the potential impact of a service or a means of service delivery. The public sector has been much less likely to market test its products than the private sector, but such testing is often necessary. Like questionnaires, experiments need to be carefully designed if we are to draw general conclusions from them. Local authorities might well make rather more use of experimentation and pilot testing than they do.

Market segmentation

Market segmentation is the process of dividing up the market into separate parts or segments. The people who will use and buy products are not a homogeneous, undifferentiated mass but are made up of groups and individuals with different needs and characteristics. There has been a move away from mass marketing to marketing targeted on specific groups. In the extreme, each individual can be treated as a separate market, but that is rarely possible in practice.

Before an organisation can decide on its detailed marketing strategy it must segment the market. There are many bases of segmentation, the most common of which are:

- Geography – patterns of consumption will vary from area to area, and organisations may choose to serve specific areas.
- Demography – markets may be divided on the basis of a number of variables such as age, sex, social class, employment status, religion or race. Demographic segmentation is frequently used because it is relatively simple and cheap to gather such information.
- Life-style – distinguishing target markets on the basis of lifestyle has become increasingly popular; it is used by the Conservative Party to determine its popularity. It is based upon psychographics, which distinguishes groups of people using the statistical technique of factor analysis. Life-style analysis has passed into the language with the use of acronyms such as yuppies and dinkies. Yuppies are young upwardly mobile professionals and dinkies are dual career couples with no children – double income, no kids.
- Product relationships – markets might be distinguished according to the

existing use of the product, for example into users and non-users, or into occasional and frequent users. For many products profit comes from getting existing users to use a product more often, not from getting new people to buy a product. Local authorities face similar problems, for example in understanding why more use is not made of educational facilities, libraries or leisure centres.

Different variables can be used to segment the market on a multi-dimensional basis using clustering techniques, for example combining demographic and geographical or user variables.

		Age	
		Old	Young
Use	User	1	2
	Non-user	3	4

Figure 3.5. Two-dimensional segmentation

It will rarely be the case that a single variable can be used adequately to analyse any particular market, especially as the world in which local authorities must operate becomes more complex.

Benefit analysis is a particularly important basis of segmentation. Services can be viewed as combinations of characteristics or features, which allow the consumer to derive a variety of benefits from the product. It is important for the marketer to know the benefits that different groups of consumers derive from a given product and which characteristics provide those benefits. For example, some might buy a particular brand of clothing because it has the right designer label, others because it is hard-wearing, and others simply because they think that it looks good. The product that was in the producer's mind may not be the product that the consumer experiences, and different groups may derive different benefits. Local authorities need to ask themselves:

▽ Which consumers get which benefits from the services that they provide?
▽ Which characteristics of the products provide those benefits?

They must consider the threefold relationship between the consumers, the benefits that they derive from products and the characteristics of the service that provide those benefits.

A further means of segmenting the market is to consider the situation in which the product will be used, and attempt to design it for the specific circumstances involved. Shoes and clothes will differ depending on whether they are for use or for ornamentation: decoration will be different in the living-room from the bedrooms. Services may be used by people who face considerable emotional and physical problems that will greatly influence the way that they can use services. Considering the situation in which a product will be used allows a clearer analysis of benefits.

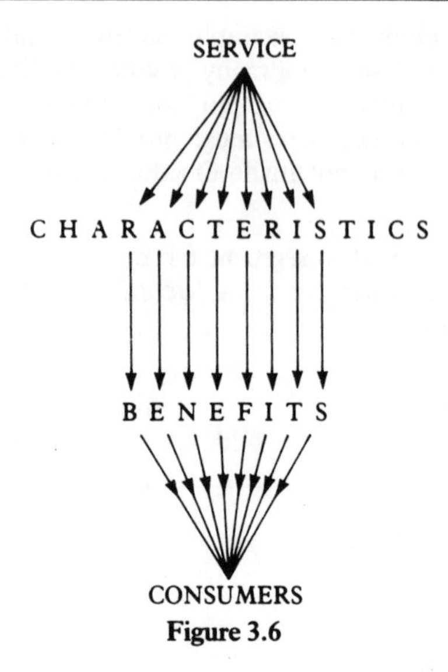

Figure 3.6

The organisation will need a targeting strategy expressing its approach to the various segments of the market. The organisation may operate on the basis of one or many services and one or many markets.

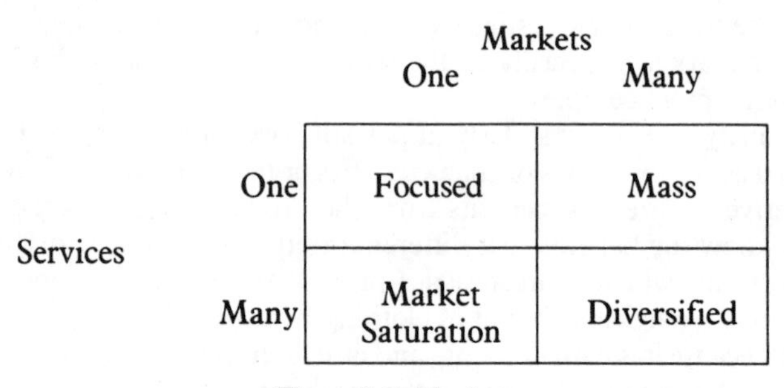

Figure 3.7. Markets

It may choose:

▽ A mass strategy – providing the same service to all segments – like Henry Ford's model T any colour as long as it is black.
▽ Producing a single service for a single segment, a highly focused strategy.
▽ Producing different services for different segments, a diversified strategy.
▽ Producing a number of services for the same segment.

Having divided up the market, and having decided on the broad strategy to be adopted, one can decide upon the market position, which refers to the relationship between the service and the market segment being served. The position of the service describes the image that it has for that segment and the way that it is used. One may decide to produce cars for the rich, but attempt to position the company specifically as the provider of the family runabout rather than the main status providing car. A cereal producer may focus upon providing healthy cereals for children. The local authority must make similar decisions, for example about the sort of housing or residential care that it provides, for example supplying high or low grade products. The approach to promotion and advertising depends upon the position that the organisation wants to adopt. The position adopted will, in turn, depend strongly on the extent of competition. Good positioning will clearly differentiate the organisation and its products from those of competitive organisations.

Segmentation, targeting and positioning become more important as the environment the organisation faces becomes more complex. The organisation can occupy one of a whole range of niches and which niche it chooses and how it is approached will determine the future of the organisation. Choosing the right niche becomes more important and more difficult as the life-cycle of products shortens and one product replaces another with greater regularity. The niches within which the organisation must survive become ever narrower as competition and complexity grow. Few products — Coca Cola, Mars Bars and Levi-Strauss jeans spring to mind — can continue relatively unchanged over generations. Most organisations must change their products regularly as tastes and technologies change. Continuity in production is a great aid to the efficiency that comes from experience and progress up the learning curve, but for effectiveness we need change and differentiation to cope with developments in demand. Many of the most important developments in production management and technology are attempts to combine flexibility and continuity.

The importance of market segmentation analysis is that it recognises the majority or average fallacy. The product that is designed to appeal to the average customer may not appeal to any specific group. It may be everybody's second choice but the one that nobody wants. Analysis of segmentation and position forces the organisation to be clear on what products they are designing for which groups and how that product will provide benefits to the user. It is important that segments be as large and accessible as possible, and that the organisation should measure the segment as accurately as possible. The two basic approaches to segmentation are either to determine which groups the organisation wishes to serve and then which benefits it wishes to deliver, or to operate by determining benefits first and groups second. In either case the situation of use can be seen as intervening between groups and benefits. Whether the service will provide the benefits intended will depend upon it being designed in a way that is appropriate to the circumstances of use.

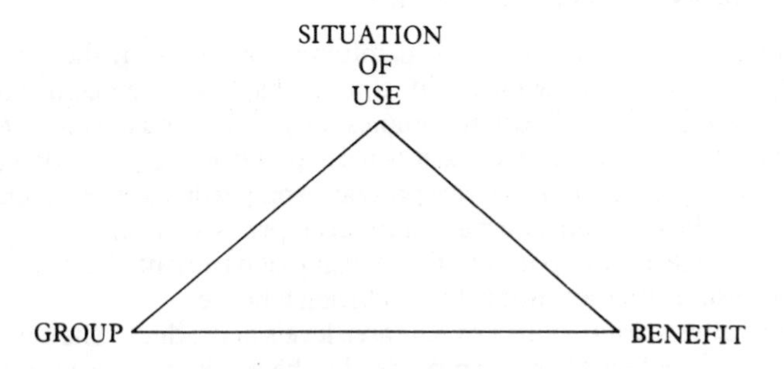

Figure 3.8. Bases of segmentation

One must always consider the situation in which the user will be when using the service and the way that it influences the benefit that the group gets from the product.

Marketing mix

The core of the marketing approach is the marketing mix, which is the specific set of tools used in attempting to satisfy a given market. It consists of the set of factors under the organisation control which it can vary to produce different marketing strategies. The most common distinction describes the marketing mix as the four P's:

- ∇ Product
- ∇ Price
- ∇ Promotion
- ∇ Place

The marketing mix is then the blend of decisions that is made about each of these variables. There will also be a mix of decisions within each of these broad variables, so that there will be a product mix, a price mix, a promotion mix and a place mix.

THE PRODUCT MIX

The nature of the product, whether service or manufactured goods, that the organisation produces is fundamental. The first decision that needs to be made is over the product range. Is the organisation to provide a narrow or a broad product range? Decisions must then be made on quality and on the use of brand names. Is the organisation to go for high grade, branded products or adopt a more generic approach? The product as experienced will also depend on after-sales and warranty. In some cases organisations expect simply to sell their product, and have no further contact with the consumer. In other cases, whether the product is satisfactory depends upon post-purchase support. The simpler the product the more the customer-producer relationship can be reduced. As Landes says of the development of the mass production of watches:

> . . . if a dollar watch ran, fine: if not, the buyer could send it back for replacement or throw it away. At low price levels, it is simpler to shift the task of quality control to the consumer.

By contrast nobody expects to buy a mainframe computer off the shelf, take it back to the office and simply plug it in. If it breaks down the manufacturer will carry some responsibility. The more complex the product and the more important it is to the consumer, the more contact is needed between organisation and consumer. This is especially so for service products and particularly in the public service where the link of consumer and producer persists through time, and the 'after-sales' service is all important. The housing department, for example, does not fulfil its responsibilities simply by producing a house.

Kotler makes a distinction between three levels of product. The core product is the essence of the benefit that is provided by the product. It answers the question 'What it is for?'. The 'tangible' product is the product as it is presented to the consumer, embodying features such as styling, packaging and branding. It is the tangible qualities of the product that will bear its identity. The 'augmented' product refers to those things that are added to the basic product, after-sales service, delivery and additional, add-on products. As industry shifts from product to system control, so the augmented product becomes more important. Products become part of larger processes, and managing the product entails managing the whole process. Local authority housing has gone through the same process and the management of housing has increased in importance compared with its production. The more complex the services provided the more attention needs to be given to all three of the product levels.

Product and product marketing must change over time because there is a product life-cycle: products are created, grow to maturity and ultimately die. Promotion and information providing will be more important in the introduction and growth periods than when the product is more mature. Pricing will be different in the period of establishing a product compared to a period of mature stable demand. The existence of product life-cycles means that organisations must divest themselves of products when they begin to decline, though, frequently, they do not. Part of the marketing strategy is determining when new products are needed and old ones should be discarded.

It is important not to think of a product purely in physical terms but rather as a set of characteristics yielding benefits. Unless this is done there will be confusion and ignorance as to why the consumer is using the product which may lead to failures in competition. Trains are not used by most people for their own sake, but because they provide transport. They may be used because they provide comfort or are fast and thereby release time for other activities. Any alternative means of transport is a potential competitor. Theatres and cinemas do not compete only with other theatres and cinemas, but with all the other ways that people might spend their leisure time. The local authority leisure centre is in competition with the television and the pub. The ways that products can substitute for each other can vary widely. Benefit analysis can help to clarify the important characteristics of the product for the consumer. As products mature they tend to become more complicated and it is more difficult to assess what benefits are being delivered. The more complex the product the more important the analysis of benefits will be.

PRICING

Product pricing has received a great deal of attention from economists, though studies have shown that managers have not taken a great deal of notice. In a simple world, with a large number of buyers and sellers, the market will decide the price for goods and services. But, in the world as we know it, the decision is more difficult. Organisations must decide price on the basis of both long and short-term considerations. Pricing is highly complex and can have many purposes. The organisation may price in order to maximise surplus or profit, either in the short or the long-term. It may price in order to recover costs, or to recover costs plus a standard mark-up. An organisation that wants to enter a particular market may buy its way in through loss-leading or predatory pricing. Organisations might price in order to maximise usage, for example by differential pricing, or may charge high prices in order to discourage demand or usage.

In setting its prices an organisation must take account of the elasticity of demand — the way that demand varies with price – and substitution effects — the extent to which people will switch to other products as the price rises. The organisation must also consider complementarity, that is the extent to which the purchaser needs to have the product to go with other products or vice versa. The sale of more cars will lead to an increase in petrol sales. The local authority may provide complementary products such as planning permissions. Increases in economic development activity may lead to greater demand for the work of the planner. The price of a product may be influenced by the importance or cost of the products that it complements.

Pricing strategy will depend upon pricing objectives. There are four particularly important pricing strategies:

- ▽ Profit-oriented strategy — for example to maximise profit or surplus.
- ▽ Cost-oriented strategy — for example to recover costs.
- ▽ Demand-oriented strategy — for example to maximise usage or to create disincentive.
- ▽ Competition-oriented strategy — for example to force entry into the market or to cripple the competition.

Research on pricing policy has shown that companies do not use highly complex pricing methods. The detailed analysis of the micro-economist is not an appropriate exercise when setting product price. Organisations need to develop relatively simple methods that are in line with their objectives.

PROMOTION MIX

Promotion covers a range of activities, notably advertising, public relations and sales. This is the area of marketing that has attracted the most criticism, partly because it is the most visible. The popular image of sales is close to confidence trickery and the butt of popular jokes. Advertising is seen as persuading people to buy products that they do not need with money that they have not got, and which are shoddy anyway. Public relations is seen as the manipulation of the media and public opinion. No doubt there is some truth in these images, but the promotion of products is necessary. In a complex world of many products it provides valuable information, and thereby reduces the time that it takes to make decisions and saving us some of the time of searching. It also helps us to make more efficient decisions by creating images between which we can decide. The value of a brand name that is well known through promotion is that we know what to buy without going through extensive processes of search and decision. The more crowded is the product world the more we need information in order to choose and the more advertising can play a role in providing it.

Advertising is largely the communication of images and information in total messages. In deciding on advertising one must distinguish between the medium, for example newspapers, television, radio or direct mail, and the message. Different media will be appropriate for different messages and more effective in reaching different groups. The growth of computerised information systems is making direct, personalised mail more possible. The message will vary depending upon the product — the more complex the product the more information will be required by the user. The advertising task is fourfold:

- ▽ To attract the attention of potential consumers.
- ▽ To interest them in the product being promoted
- ▽ To arouse in them a desire for the product
- ▽ To spur them to take action and buy the product.

In fulfilling these tasks the advertiser must think about how the potential consumer will experience the advertisements. Typically the advertiser will emphasise a characteristic of the product, a benefit that will derive from that product and why the consumer would want that benefit. For example, added crystals in a soap powder will provide a bluer white and create a happy family.

The effectiveness of advertising is not well understood. Crude, propagandistic, notions are obviously untrue. People will not rush out and buy a product just because they have seen an advertisement for it. Perhaps the most important influence of advertising is its effect upon our general understanding of the world. Many studies have shown how advertising reinforces stereotypes and presents a simplified view of the world. Before using advertising local authorities will need to ensure that its form fits with their political and social values.

Public relations is concerned with communicating information to those outside the organisation and creating and maintaining relationships with other organisations and individuals. It is often a low level function, reacting to, rather than initiating events. But as the world has become more complex so public relations has come to play a larger part. For politicians public relations has become particularly important. Public relations involves more specific strategies of communication than advertising and more precise targeting of the message. Relations with the press and other news media are a particularly important part of public relations, for the organisation's image and reputation will be influenced as much by general press coverage as by advertisements, which will always be suspected of partiality. The growing importance of links between organisations means that public relations must be more than simply massaging the tired and bruised image of the organisation. Public relations professionals will not only be a link between the organisation and the outside world, but also with other organisations. Their job will also be to develop a public relations strategy for the organisation as a whole and help others to communicate more effectively.

Sales is sometimes confused with the whole of marketing, rather than being seen as a small part of it, which is not surprising given that sales is often the most visible part of the marketing function. The need for sales will be reduced the more effective is the rest of the marketing function. The better designed and targeted the product the less effort is needed to sell it. But, however good the product, a totally passive approach will fail; it is no use having an excellent product if nobody is aware of the fact. Products may fail, however good they are, because they are sold ineffectively. The sales function is a crucial link to the outside world for many organisations.

Sales has two essential functions: to persuade and enable people to get the product; and to act as an intermediary between the organisation and its customers. The more complex a product is the more it will need good selling. Customers will want to know a good deal about how complicated products work and what problems they will face in using them. Sales people will be required to have a degree of technical expertise and to maintain the link between the organisation and its clients and its customers. Good sales people have been found to have a number of characteristics:

- They are persuasive not critical.
- They are intuitive not analytical.
- They have high average energy levels.
- They are motivated by power, prestige and personal gain, not service.

The introduction of good sales people may lead to clashes with a service ethic, as the experience of some direct labour organisations has shown. Local authorities will certainly need to approach the world of sales with care.

The promotion mix is more important the more developed and sophisticated the product being marketed and the wider the range of products. It describes the strategy that the organisation has for external communication. The greater the interest of the press, radio and television in the organisation, the more important it is to have a clear promotional strategy. Promotion should, preferably, be positive, aimed to shape and develop the image that the organisation wishes to project, rather than simply react to external forces. Kotler summarises the characteristic of good publicity:

- ▽ Credible: news may be more credible than advertisements.
- ▽ Off-guard: good publicity tells people things that they did not expect to hear.
- ▽ Dramatisation: good promotion may add dramatic effect to the product.

A clear promotion strategy can serve to establish a clear relationship between the organisation and its market.

PLACE

The fourth element of the marketing mix is the distribution of the product, for which 'place' is the shorthand. Having produced a material product, the organisation must consider the use of wholesale and retail outlets or direct provision in order to ensure that it reaches the customers. The term commonly used to refer to this process is 'channels of distribution', and includes the transportation of the product, and problems of storage and inventory management. Innovation and developments in the channelling of products have been as important as new products themselves in changing our patterns of consumption. Refrigeration, for example, changed our patterns of food consumption by allowing the long-distance transportation of food, while rapid public transport changed shopping patterns, which are being changed again by car ownership. Advances in information technology have changed the nature of the holiday trade as sophisticated booking and control systems become possible. Distribution costs are important, often representing 15–20% of sales turnover. In local government the debate about decentralisation is essentially a debate about place — about the channels by which services are distributed.

Power is a key dimension in the relationship with the marketing channel, and will vary with the nature of the product and the pattern of demand. Where products can be stored much of the power will lie with the wholesaler and to a lesser extent the retailer. Where stockpiling is not possible then the producer, or the supplier of new materials will be dominant. Industrial battles are often based on such patterns of power and influence. Before the miners' strike the Government ensured that there were large stockpiles of coal; the past power of the Fleet Street print workers was based on the fact that they could destroy the most perishable of products. The distribution system also involves different approaches to dealing with risk. By maintaining stocks, or ensuring a rapid delivery system, we can reduce the risk to the producer of losing sales, and to the consumer of not being able to get hold of the products they want.

The chain of linkages:

Manufacturer — Wholesaler — Retailer — Consumer

is a chain of power and risk. It is also a chain of quality, which can break down at any point. Integration is one way in which the organisation can try to influence the chain of distribution. Retailers may integrate backward into manufacturing, buying up the production capacity, or producers may integrate forward buying a retailing capacity. Producers or retailers may reduce the uncertainty they face by these processes of vertical integration. Where they do not integrate backwards or forwards, organisations may take other steps to gain control. Only certain distributors may be licensed to sell a product. Large retailers, like Marks and Spencer, may exert great influence over suppliers for whom they are the major customer, specifying very closely the materials that are to be provided. Managing distribution means managing the set of organisations through which distribution takes place.

The key aspects of distribution for the consumer are location and accessibility, which may be complex matters involving travel, local geography and the abilities of the consumer. Local authorities are having to consider these matters as they attempt to develop decentralisation. Accessibility must be considered over the long term. People may be willing to travel to shopping centres on a Saturday that they would not be willing to use at other times in the week. Distribution will have a time dimension. Managing the consumer will be a part of managing the delivery system since one must consider he or she can be enabled to use the product.

Channels of distribution will also vary with the nature of the product. Consumer products may be divided into convenience, preference, shopping and speciality goods. Convenience goods are those that are needed or wanted every day and need saturation distribution, for example through newsagents, bakeries or diaries. Preference goods are those bought regularly and routinely, requiring widespread distribution, for example toiletries. Shopping goods are those on which the buyer is willing to spend some time, such as household appliances, for which distribution will be selective. Speciality goods are those which are bought rarely, such as cars, to which the consumer is willing to devote a great deal of effort, and which are likely to be bought through exclusive outlets.

Approaches to the distribution of products is changing because of new technology and because new distribution systems are being developed. New technology has made possible the development of more sophisticated systems of purchasing and stockholding systems. Warehouses are increasingly automated. New systems of distribution are being created by franchising, rental and leasing systems. These approaches are particularly important in the development of services marketing and they are being used extensively by local authorities, for example through the leasing of capital equipment.

Two dimensions can be used to describe the overall pattern of distribution of goods and services:

- ▽ Concentration/dispersion – it is possible to have a highly concentrated pattern of distribution in which the consumer must come to the organisation, or to have many delivery sites.
- ▽ Integrated/independent – where the process of distribution can affect the consumer's experience the producer will want to be able to influence the distribution process. The more important distribution is to the organisation the more likely it is that distribution will be integrated with the producing organisation.

Local authorities must consider both of these dimensions, for example in the development of decentralisation or competitive tendering.

Marketing, philosophy and technique

Marketing is more philosophy than specific skill. It draws on a range of disciplines and techniques. Strategic marketing draws upon the planning and decision-making literature. Consumer research draws upon various aspects of psychology and sociology. Economics and accounting theory also provide the theoretical underpinnings for work on distribution or pricing. Operations research may be used in designing systems of distribution. Highly sophisticated techniques have been used in analysing markets, for example factor analysis in segmenting markets, or repertory grid and cluster techniques in analysing consumer preferences. Few organisations will be large enough to employ people skilled in each area of marketing, and outside agencies are frequently used, for example in advertising.

The sum of the various techniques that can be used does not give us a total picture of what marketing is. Rather it is a philosophy that implies a recognition of the relationship between the consumer and the organisation. It recognises that the economic theory of the market, with its emphasis on well defined products, instantaneous adjustment and perfect knowledge, bears little relationship to reality. The marketing philosophy recognises that both product and consumer, and the relationship between them, are complex.

Conclusion

Marketing is a combination of strategy and of understanding the consumer. In this chapter I have examined the strategic aspects of marketing. I have presented the major elements that go to make up the marketing strategy, particularly market segmentation and the marketing mix. In each of these elements the degree of sophistication can be considerable, but the marketing process should not be seen as the preserve of the marketing experts alone. The decisions that are made in a marketing strategy are fundamental decisions about the nature of the business that the organisation is in and how it goes about conducting that business.

Questions and Exercises

▲ 1. *What dimensions would be most appropriate for analysing the portfolio of services that you wish to provide in your service?*

▲ 2. *Is a defensive approach, of sticking to existing services and existing target markets, the right approach for local authorities generally and for your service in particular?*

▲ 3. *Consider the following method of research:*
desk research
collection of statistical data
telephone surveys
postal surveys
structured interviews
unstructured interviews
observation

Which would be most appropriate for investigating the following?

Problem	***Method of Research***
Why children fail to attend school	
Failure to take up social security benefits	
Underuse of libraries	
High levels of litter in the town centre	
How to improve the take-up of public transport	
Assessing satisfaction with provision in parks	
The level of use of neighbourhood offices	
High levels of rent arrears	

▲ 4. *What are the most appropriate determinants of segmentation for your service?*

▲ 5. *What benefits does your service or services provide to those whom it serves? Which characteristics of the services that you provide are related to which benefits?*

▲ 6. *What dimensions would you use to describe the position that you take in your service, for example are you engaged in mass marketing or more precise targeting?*

▲ 7. *Consider a marketing problem that you have in your service or your authority. Is it:*

a problem of market segmentation
a problem of market position
a problem of the nature of the product
a problem of price
a problem of promotion
a problem of place?

▲ 8. *What are the major elements of the marketing mix for your service?*

4 The consumer perspective

Key points

- ▲ *The nature of the consumption process: the reasons for use, the decision to use, the use of the product, post-usage evaluation.*
- ▲ *The way in which consumer decisions are made — rational processes and behavioural approaches.*
- ▲ *The influence of the situation of use.*
- ▲ *The importance of risk, involvement and effort.*
- ▲ *Use and service quality.*
- ▲ *Complaints — the failure of complaints procedures and the positive use of complaints.*
- ▲ *The process of communicating with consumers.*

The essence of marketing is to understand the consumer. It is no good having a brilliant, innovative product if nobody wants to buy it; the evidence seems to be that if you build a better mousetrap people will not necessarily beat a path to your door. They need to know about it and want it. You must market the product. Of course we may be able to force people to use our products, or persuade them to do so through manipulative advertising. But again the evidence is that these strategies will have limited value. Ogilvy, the popular philosopher of advertising, argues that:

> The average family is now exposed to more than 1500 advertisements a day. No wonder they have acquired a talent for skipping the advertisements in newspapers and magazines, and going to the bathroom during television commercials.

If an organisation is to succeed it must, in the words of Peters and Waterman, be close to the customer, and provide services that people want. Good advertising will rarely compensate for a poor product.

If we want to attain this closeness to the customer then we must consider the stages involved in the process of consumption, namely:

- ▽ The reasons for purchase.
- ▽ The choice or purchase process.
- ▽ The usage of the product.
- ▽ Post-usage evaluation.

Marketing is concerned with each of these stages. The majority of study has gone into the actual purchase decision, because that is the most identifiable stage, but all the stages are important. One cannot treat consumers as if they are just first-time users for in most cases we will be dealing with repeat usage. It is the relationship with the consumer through time that we are concerned with.

The reasons for use may be various. We may use a product, whether it is a good or a service:

▽ To solve a specific problem.
▽ To prevent a problem arising.
▽ For symbolic purposes.
▽ Out of habit.
▽ Because of persuasion.
▽ Because we are forced to.

The more complex the product, the more varied the reasons for which we may purchase it. In some cases we will use goods or services because we are forced to, either there are legal requirements or because we have no realistic choice, for example in using water. Reasons for use will change over time. Goods initially bought because they give pleasure may over time become necessities without which we will not be comfortable. Few would now see telephones, televisions or refrigerators as luxuries. Reasons for use are likely to be many, even in the case of a single product, for each product is a collection of characteristics, meeting different needs and wants, and providing a number of benefits.

The purchase decision has been at the core of marketing analysis and has been the subject of a great deal of psychological study. Many of the key areas of psychology — memory, cognitive structures and perception amongst others — have been used to explain the way that people make the purchasing decision. But the various approaches can be divided into two broad groups:

▽ Rational approaches.
▽ Behavioural approaches.

I will argue that both are necessary to some degree if we are to understand why people act as they do towards different products in different circumstances.

Rational explanations of consumer behaviour

Rational approaches have dominated. A simple model is that the physical and social world will affect a person's attitudes, which will be expressed in action. Our behaviour expresses our psychological constitution. Attitudes are certainly viewed, both by laypeople and by psychologists, as crucial determinants of behaviour. But the relationship between attitudes and action is not simple and direct. There may well be a gap between attitudes and behaviour as a number of classical psychological experiments have shown. The most famous is that of Lapiere who, in the United States in the 1930s, found that many hotel owners, who said that they would not accommodate Chinese people, did so in practice. Equally those who said that they would accommodate Chinese people did not. The study has been the subject of much debate and criticism, but the fundamental argument that attitudes and actions are not the same has persisted. Many later studies have shown that we cannot predict action from a simple and crude knowledge of attitudes. Knowing peoples attitudes does not tell us how they will behave.

One of the most influential models of the relationship between attitude and action is that of Ajzen and Fishbein, who argue that behaviour is related closely to the intention to act, and that one can predict behaviour from intentions. The determinants of intentions are:

- ▽ Attitude towards the behaviour: whether we are positive or negative towards the behaviour.
- ▽ Subjective norms: the evaluation of the social pressures that exist for us to behave in one way rather than another.

Attitudes are in turn a function of beliefs about whether performing a given behaviour will have a positive or a negative result:

> . . . a person who believes that performing a given behaviour will lead to mostly positive outcomes will hold a favourable attitude towards performing that behaviour . . .

Such a model implies that behaviour is the outcome of a complex relationship between intentions, norms, beliefs and attitudes.

It is not possible to predict specific behaviour from generalised attitudes. Local authorities are not likely to learn much about how people will behave from general surveys about satisfaction or dissatisfaction with services. If we wish to predict and influence behaviour then we must specify that behaviour closely and study attitudes, norms and intentions related to that specific behaviour. If we wish to predict whether people will wear seatbelts then it is no good asking generalised questions about attitudes towards seatbelts or road safety. If we wish to stop people dropping litter then we should not base our actions on generalised attitudes towards litter. We may need to consider whether they will drop litter in one circumstance but not in another. For example, people may drop litter when they feel that there is already a great deal of litter for which they are not to blame but would not litter unlittered areas. They may be against dropping litter but feel that their action in doing so will make no appreciable difference to the actual level of litter. People may easily perform specific actions that clash with generalised attitudes. We need to ask about and study the circumstances in which people will and will not drop litter or wear seatbelts. In order to understand how people will act in different situations we will need a great deal of information.

It is difficult to change attitudes and values. One consumer behaviour textbook argues:

> As a general rule it can be stated that the best strategy is to accept strongly held evaluative criteria as given and make modifications in the marketing mix where necessary to match company offerings with consumer specifications (Engel et al. 1963).

More simply it may be best to take people as we find them. This premise will have strong implications for local government, which is often concerned with basic and deeply held attitudes and values.

Most of us are searching for an environment that allows us to operate with relatively simple mental structures that have a degree of balance and enable us to hold a positive view of ourselves. This is especially so in the case of services that involve us as people, rather than goods that are simply things that we live with. Individuals will differ in their tolerance of, and liking for, complexity, and some will make finer distinctions between situations than others, but all need some stability. None of us can operate continually with the need to make highly complex decisions, and cope with unending uncertainty. Part of the process of marketing services is to ensure that the demands that we are making on people are not too great, and to try to make it easier to make the better decision. For example, we can site litter-bins so that people do not have to make efforts or decisions not to drop litter. We can, more generally, design services so that they are pleasant and easy to use.

Behaviour

A second approach to predicting the way that consumers will act has been based upon the study of behaviour rather than rational processes and the influence of attitudes. It is based upon the idea that it is better to try to change behaviour rather than to try to influence the attitudes or values that people hold. Our immediate reaction may be to reject such an idea because it fits ill with our conceptions of ourselves as conscious, rational beings, rather than mechanistic organisms. It can be seen as having overtones of manipulation. But a little reflection will persuade us that things are a little more complex than that; we are often unclear about why we act as we do, and about what our attitudes and emotions are. We frequently rationalise our attitudes and beliefs so that they fit with the way that we prefer to behave, and deep-seated behaviour may easily clash with the way that we would like to act.

The origins of the approach to explaining consumer behaviour by focusing on action lie in behavioural theory. The simplest approach is to explain actions in terms of stimulus-response mechanisms. Pavlov found that the relationship between stimulus and response could be manipulated to product a response with a secondary stimulus. A stimulus, such as meat to a dog, will produce a response of salivation; a second stimulus, a bell, can be coupled with the first and, eventually come to replace it, actually producing the response on its own. The dog can be made to salivate on the ringing of a bell. This is the process of classical conditioning. A second approach 'operant conditioning' waits for a desired response to be produced and reinforces it through reward, producing a bias for that sort of action in the future.

Behaviour conditioning theory implies that we can influence people so that they react automatically in the way that we want them to given the appropriate stimulus. Classical conditioning ideas lie behind the playing of music in stores, the different colours used in packaging goods, the use of famous people to endorse products or the sponsorship of sport. Detailed work has been done on these subjects, for example studies of the pace of music in stores has shown that people tend to spend more when slow music is played because they walk more slowly and spend more time in the store.

More complex behavioural theories have been developed. Bem, for example, argues that we come to know our attitudes through inferring them from our behaviour. Modifying behaviour can serve to modify attitudes. This is not a particularly surprising idea if we consider the way that children come to learn the meaning of their behaviour. We often act and then have to interpret what we meant by our actions. The behavioural studies of consumer behaviour and decision-making would suggest that if we want to change peoples' attitudes and values then we might do so by changing the environment in which they operate, or acting directly to change the way that they behave.

People and situations

The decisions that we take on purchasing goods or using services are likely to be influenced by our attitudes and the circumstances in which we find ourselves. In some situations we will act according to routine and habit, in others we will act in a rational and considered way. Much of the time we neither need nor want to spend time on deliberation; automatic reaction will be more efficient. Much of our everyday behaviour is automatic; it would be impossible to get through the day if this were not so. It would be impossible for our every action to be the result of a conscious thought-out decision, or life would become an intolerable, unending, series of decisions. Whether we make a conscious decision or not will depend largely on the nature of the activity involved and the circumstances in which it takes place.

It is useful to think about the way that we make decisions in terms of the internal mental structures and schemes that we use to make sense of our experience and actions. These form more or less habitualised routines that do not make great demands of us. More generally we may think of decisions at three levels of uncertainty:

- ▽ The application of well-developed schemes that are more or less routine and involve little or no conscious thought.
- ▽ Situations that do not fit into patterned schemes but which can be interpreted within them given certain basic adjustments.
- ▽ Completely unfamiliar situations for which our existing patterned understandings are completely useless and for which we need a whole new set of structures.

The first type of situation might be represented by catching a bus and paying the fare; the second by going out to a formal dinner for the first time; the third by losing your job and being thrown on the dole. Different levels of challenge to our everyday understandings will be presented by each of these levels of uncertainty. Catching a bus, as long as we have done it before, will involve largely automatic actions. Attending a formal dinner may demand new behaviour and therefore decisions. Being thrown on the dole may demand decisions but we may lack the structure within which to make those decisions. Local government managers might consider what sort of mental structure their service will demand from those who use it. At each level our decision will be a mixture of the behavioural and the rational. The situation or the person may dominate in any given circumstance.

Which factor dominates a given decision — situation or person will depend to a great extent upon character and personality though these in turn will be shaped by the environment. Those who attribute outcomes to the external world, over which they see themselves as having little influence, will react differently from those who attribute them to their own actions. The reaction to unemployment, whether active or passive, depends partly upon whether one blames oneself or external forces. Those who blame the world are likely to react more passively. The result is often self-fulfilling prophecy, where any feelings that I will fail will reduce my motivation to succeed, leading to failure and reinforcement of my feeling or failure. These processes are very important in the public sector, where many of those who use services are in a powerless and disadvantaged position. The experience that they have may well reinforce helplessness if we do not give careful attention to the behavioural aspects of a service as the users experience it.

Much of the concern of the local authority must be to change the way that people react to circumstances.

Consumer decisions, then, are the result both of conscious action, either more or less routine, and situationally determine behaviour. Different levels of conscious action and pre-determined behaviour will dominate different choices. Some choices are more the result of conscious rational action, others the result of circumstances. There are three main factors that will determine the level of conscious involvement in any given consumer decision:

▽ Risk.
▽ Involvement.
▽ Effort.

Broadly, the greater the risk, the greater the involvement and the greater the effort that is involved in the use of a good or service the more likely and the more necessary is rational decision-making.

RISK, INVOLVEMENT AND EFFORT

Consumer decisions involve risk. The product may fail completely, it may not be fit for its purpose, or it may involve financial commitment and risk when we use it, and thereby pre-empt other choices. At the extreme we are risking our lives, through buying dangerous cars or dangerous drugs. In most decisions, the level of risk is not high, but large decisions always involve some element of risk since we are committing our resources to one line of action and therefore pre-empting another. Risk varies directly with the resources committed. The greater the risk the more difficult and stressful a decision will be. Consumers, in making decisions, will generally act to minimise the risk.

Some products involve us more than others because they are more important to our lives and to us as human beings. High involvement products are those that make a difference to how we see ourselves or how others see us, that will have a strong and perceptible impact upon the way that we live our lives, or that are important to us for other reasons. Involvement will vary with the social, moral and political values of the individual. For some, clothes and personal appearance will be all important, for others the food that they eat or the car they drive will take on greater significance. Few people care very much about the brand of salt they use, most people care deeply about the house they live in. Buying salt will not involve us, buying houses will. Brand names for routine products perform the function of preventing us from having to make detailed choices, as in the case of washing powders. We can buy in a non-involved way by simply responding to the stimulus provided by the brand. For even simpler products branding itself may be unnecessary. The less involving the product, the happier we are likely to be with generic branding. High involvement products such as cars are not likely to be of generic brands. We can, therefore, distinguish between products that are highly involving and those that involve us little. The most important, high involvement products are not likely to be susceptible to pre-packaging and branding but will often be custom made. Intermediate products may be branded, but even this may not be necessary for products that involve us very little.

Consumer decisions will involve effort and the investment of resources. We may have to search, physically or in terms of information, for the product that we want. We may have to make more mental effort to understand the dimensions and elements involved in the decision. We may have to test a host of different products to ensure that we are getting what we want. We will be willing to exert much more effort in deciding on purchases of products that are more important to us.

The degree of effort, risk and involvement will all vary with the level of resources that a person has, and with the nature of the service. For the rich, the choice of goods is a less risky business. They can more easily afford to put mistakes right, and product failure is less important. Indeed, for the very rich, daily life may become so devoid of risk that there is a search for areas of danger, in the casino or on the stock exchange. For the poor most products carry a great risk because the failure even of simple day-to-day goods and service can have a great impact. A major difficulty for the poor is that they must often buy in the less reliable second-hand market where the quality of goods is harder to assess and less subject to guarantee, and the risk of failure is greater. Effort is also related to resources in that the less resources we have the more we must strive to make sure that we use them well. Involvement patterns will vary with wealth in that the rich will attach less importance to the everyday necessities of life, such as food and heating, which will be crucial, highly involving matters for the poor. For the rich the crucial commodity will be time as those firms that market 'time management' know well. The richer you are the more the problem of consumption becomes one of finding time to engage in all the consumption that is possible.

The nature of the product will also influence our perception of risk effort and involvement. Expensive products are likely to be high on all three, because they involve our ideas of ourselves as people. Those products that most obviously give us pleasure are more likely to involve us, so much that the process of choice is one that we enjoy. Most of us enjoy shopping for records, clothes or jewellery. By contrast we do not enjoy the process of choice when it is difficult and hard to understand, as in the case of house buying, when most of us feel uncertain and the prisoners of fate.

The process that we go through to make choices will be different for different products and will depend on our resources because of the different levels of risk, involvement and effort that different products require. We will gather information on different products in different ways. Kasserjian has argued that there are broadly two ways in which messages are received from the media. The first, the direct route, involves the direct perception of the message, the second, the indirect route, involves only subconscious action. Subsequent theory has developed this argument proposing that there are different types of memory and processes of persuasion. This work has been specifically related to involvement with the product, so that information about high involvement products is likely to follow the direct route. More generally one would expect that products associated with high risk, involvement and effort are more likely to invoke conscious processes of choice and reaction. Some products are so simple that they will make almost no demands upon us, others so complex that the decision can be emotionally and physically draining. Low risk, low involvement products are likely to elicit little consumer effort, leading to habitual response.

Consumers and use

We choose products for a purpose, even if that purpose is one of symbolic display. Consumer satisfaction will depend upon product quality, which is a measure of whether it is fit for its purpose. It may be that all consumption except the most routine leads to dissatisfaction because we continually raise our psychological sights. The purpose of consumption and the satisfaction we gain from it may well change over time. We must evaluate consumer satisfaction both in the immediate use and over time to reflect changing tastes and expectations. It is not only the development of new products that will cause change but the spontaneous inherent dynamic of consumption itself. As we shall see, this poses special problems for local government and the public services.

In evaluating a product that is in use we are essentially concerned with quality, which is not simply a matter of whether there are defects. We might consider a product to be of poor quality if we did not think that it fitted the purpose, even though it might fit an ill-judged specification. The first aspect of quality is conformance with the specification but the second is fitness for purpose. The local authority must not only ensure that the service is up to specification but also that it fulfils the purpose that it is supposed to fulfil. The first of these requirements is met by quality control procedures and the second by quality assurance. Quality control involves checking products and services after they have been produced to ensure that they reach the required standard. Quality assurance is an attempt to ensure that quality products or services are produced in the first place. Quality control involves trying to inspect quality in goods and services, quality assurance is trying to build quality into the production process. One can ask of a service, as does the National Consumer Council, not only:

> Does it do what it is supposed to?

but also:

> Does it do what it is not supposed to?

A stove may cook, but it may also use great quantities of gas and electricity because it is inefficient. One can then go on to ask a further series of questions, for example:

- ▽ What is it like to use?
- ▽ Is it reliable?
- ▽ How durable is it?

In designing a service we need to know the questions that people will ask in assessing it.

Consumer satisfaction must also be measured continuously, especially for high involvement products where one is likely to be buying a system through time rather than use at single moment. Satisfaction with the education service, the social services or the housing service is not likely to be decided by the experience of the moment. The aim of the producer of the service is to generate satisfaction so as to ensure commitment over time. Consumer satisfaction will also change over time as other products become available, either as substitutes or complements.

Complaints and complaining

Organisations tend to hear the good news about themselves. Few of us will easily hear the message that we ourselves are failing, and organisations are no different. There is a vicious spiral in which complaints are systematically filtered out of the system which in turn leads to more complaints, none of which surface in the organisation.

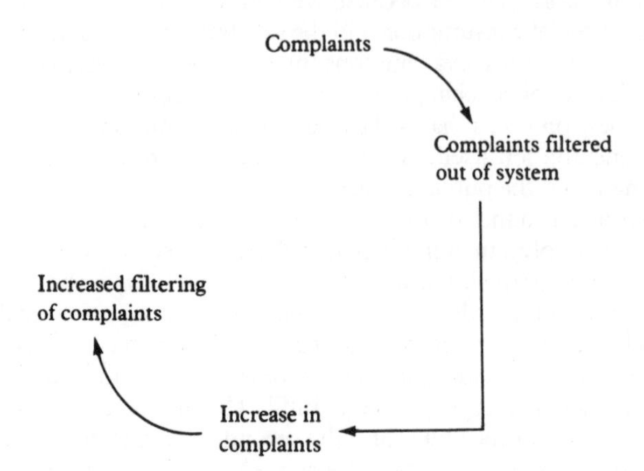

Figure 4.1. The vicious cycle of complaints

Alternatively local authorities may rationalise complaints as the result of the ignorance of the user compared to the professional or to problems outside their control such as lack of resources. Those who complain may be stereotyped as malcontents.

No doubt complaints are not always a measure of the quality of performance. They may be unjustified. There are to be sure professional complainers. But dissatisfaction should be a matter of concern to the authority and a key measure of performance. In fact local authorities make relatively little use of complaints systems with many authorities having no system at all, and even those that do rarely using them positively as a source of information about the quality of the service that they are providing. Complaints systems can play a valuable part in the market research process.

There is another more important reasons why complaints must be taken seriously and that is that negative statements about services have more effect on consumers than positive. This is not to argue that 'knocking copy' is particularly profitable, for research shows that people evaluate messages according to the partiality of the source. Judgements from impartial sources are taken more seriously. The fact that the organisation does not systematically listen to complaints will not mean that others do not hear them. Negative evaluations circulate more rapidly and affect more people than positive. It is much easier to destroy than to create reputations.

It is dangerous to assume that everything is well on the grounds that one has not heard otherwise especially when there are no clear means to complain. The lack of obvious complaint especially in a system that makes little provision for it is hardly a measure of success. Research in the United States has shown that:

▽ The average business never hears from 96% of its unhappy customers.
▽ For every complaint there are 26 problems, 6 of which are serious.
▽ Complainers are more likely than non-complainers to do business with the organisation again even if the problem is not satisfactorily sorted out.
▽ Of those who register a complaint, between 54 and 70% will do business with the organisation again if the complaint is resolved: 96% will do so if it is resolved quickly.

- ▽ The average person with a bad consumer experience tells 9 or 10 others.
- ▽ Those who have complained and had their complaint resolved tell 5 others.

No doubt these figures will vary in different circumstances and for different products, but in themselves they illustrate the need to treat complaints positively. Dealing with dissatisfaction can be a positive way of promoting the organisation.

Communicating with consumers

The process of communicating with consumers in an age in which we are all overloaded with information is difficult. Baker argues that people are exposed to 1500 messages a day and that they only hear nine. Communication has a number of dimensions:

- ▽ Sender.
- ▽ Receiver.
- ▽ Message.
- ▽ Medium.

There will not necessarily be a direct route from sender to receiver. Berelson and his colleagues developed the two-step flow theory of communication while studying American election campaigns in the 1940's. They argued that information is often interpreted for people by opinion leaders, rather than being received directly. There are two steps rather than one between sender and receiver. Later studies of the communication process have shown that the two-step flow theory applies more to some goods and services than others and in some circumstances more than others. The deeper our involvement with a product the more likely we are to listen to direct communication. Different products and different segments of the market will demand different methods of promotion.

Different media are appropriate for different messages and for different consumers. A range of media are available.

- ▽ Television and radio.
- ▽ Newspapers, magazines and periodicals.
- ▽ Direct mail.
- ▽ Word-of-mouth.
- ▽ Use of sales people.
- ▽ Posters, billboards.

Reaching the target audience will require careful planning, especially when there is limited finance for promotion. Television, radio or general newspaper advertising may reach a large audience but for specific groups specialist periodicals may be more effective. For highly targeted promotion direct mail may be best. Billboards and posters are only likely to be useful for conveying simple messages with no specific target group.

The impact of messages varies, first, with the nature of the source. If the source of the message is highly credible it is less likely to change positive attitudes but more likely to change negative ones. Messages are also more likely to be effective if they reach those who need them and when they are seen as following from reality rather than the needs of the persuader. Advertising is more effective if it attempts to reinforce attitudes rather than to change them.

Communication with the users of services is difficult. We often have no very clear picture of who they are or of why they are using the service. It is not easy to institute promotional campaigns with very limited funds. But if local authorities are to develop better services that respond more directly to people's needs then they will need to develop better methods of communicating with those who use their services and, perhaps more importantly, those who do not.

Conclusion

The consumer perspective lies at the basis of marketing. Products need to be designed from the consumer's point of view, not the producer's. The process of consumer choice is complex: we cannot presume that the decision to purchase or use products is wholly rational. Only by painful intellectual contortions can economists maintain the myth of the rational person, given such behaviour as smoking, drug-taking, or, on the positive side, altruism. In this chapter I have argued that the decision to consume or use will depend on both rational and non-rational factors, depending on the consumer, the product and the situation.

Consumption is a process that takes place through time and which involves continuing commitments. Only the most fly-by-night operators can give no thought to future relations with the consumer. In most cases there will be a continuing set of transactions with the consumer. Both consumer and producer must have an eye to the nature of the relationship.

Questions and exercises

▲ 1. *For which of the services that you provide are those who use the service likely to be making conscious decisions or reacting automatically?*

▲ 2. *Consider the following services. Will the form of decision making tend to be rational or is it more likely to be automatic?*

	Rational	*Automatic*
Primary education		
Secondary education		
Public parks		
Public transport		
Refuse collection		
Parking facilities		
Public libraries		
Roads		
Social services		
Housing		

▲ 3. *List what you would consider to be service situations in which rational decisions are more likely, and others in which people are more likely to react automatically.*

▲ 4. *Is your service high or low on risk, involvement and effort? Consider the services listed in question 2 above: for each one consider whether the degree of risk, involvement and effort are likely to be high or low. Consider the way that risk, involvement and effort will vary for the same services for different groups of users.*

▲ 5. *What are the forms of communication that are best suited to your service?*

▲ 6. *What would constitute an efficient and effective complaints procedure for your service? How might complaints be used to tell you about your service?*

▲ 7. *Think about a service experience that you have had recently that was good.*
What was it that people did that made it good?
How were you made to feel?

▲ 8. *Think about a consumer experience that you have had recently that was bad.*
What was it that people did that made it bad?
How were you made to feel?

▲ 9. *How do you think people are made to feel by your service?*

Part III
The local government context

Introduction

The application of marketing techniques in local government is at an early stage of development. Some authorities have appointed marketing officers, established marketing departments and conducted market research. Most have made few if any moves in relation to marketing. In this part of the book I shall:

▽ Discuss the development of marketing in local authorities.
▽ Consider how the concepts that have been developed in marketing might be applied in local authorities.

I have argued that marketing does have relevance to local authorities. But we must recognise that local government has its own character to which the marketing approach must be adapted. A major characteristic of the local authority, in addition to the features that were discussed in chapter 2, is that it is largely concerned with the delivery of services which require a quite different pattern of management and marketing from manufactured goods. In this part of the book I shall start by considering the nature of services. I shall then go on to consider the way that marketing is being approached and might be developed in local authorities.

5 Marketing services

Key points

- ▲ *The distinction between primary, secondary and tertiary goods.*
- ▲ *Services as part of a continuum with material goods.*
- ▲ *Distinguishing between services and manufactured goods – the result of intangibility.*
- ▲ *The importance of consumer involvement in the production of services.*
- ▲ *The nature of the service interaction.*
- ▲ *Services as dramas.*
- ▲ *Managing the consumer.*

In simple societies the economy is organised around the production of the basic material necessities of life: food, clothing and shelter. There is neither the time nor the resources to consider any other activities. But as the economy advances and techniques progress, so new wants and needs emerge, and new products are developed. In the early industrial economy, following the industrial revolution, these new products were largely material goods, produced by manufacturing industries. These two are largely distinguished as the primary and secondary sectors of the economy:

- ▽ Primary sector: agriculture, forestry and fishing.
- ▽ Secondary sector: manufacturing and construction industries.

Now a tertiary, service, sector has emerged which employs more people than the primary and secondary sectors put together and which is the fastest growing part of the economy. Distinctions can be made within the tertiary sector into what some would call quaternary and quinary sectors, distinguishing between public services, personal services and services to industry.

There is no clear and accepted definition of services. Stanton develops the following definition:

> Services are those separately identifiable essentially intangible activities that provide want-satisfaction, and that are not necessarily tied to the sale of a product or another service. To produce a service may or may not require the use of tangible goods. However, when such use is required, there is no transfer of title (permanent ownership) to these tangible goods (Quoted by Cowell)

I shall examine some aspects of this definition below, but Alfred Marshall's statement captures the essence of a service more succinctly.

> Goods that pass out of existence at the moment of creation.

The emphemeral nature of service makes it important to get things right first time, and means that the front-line staff of the authority are the crucial determinants of quality.

In fact no all encompassing definition of services is possible because they cannot be separated from the rest of the economy. The primary and secondary sectors of the economy cannot function without the support of financial or transport services. Material goods have aspects of service built into them. They are as we have argued made up of sets of characteristics that yield a set of benefits. There is no straightforward distinction between what are goods and what are services, but a continuum from pure material goods to the most ephemeral of services. Shostack has produced the following continuum:

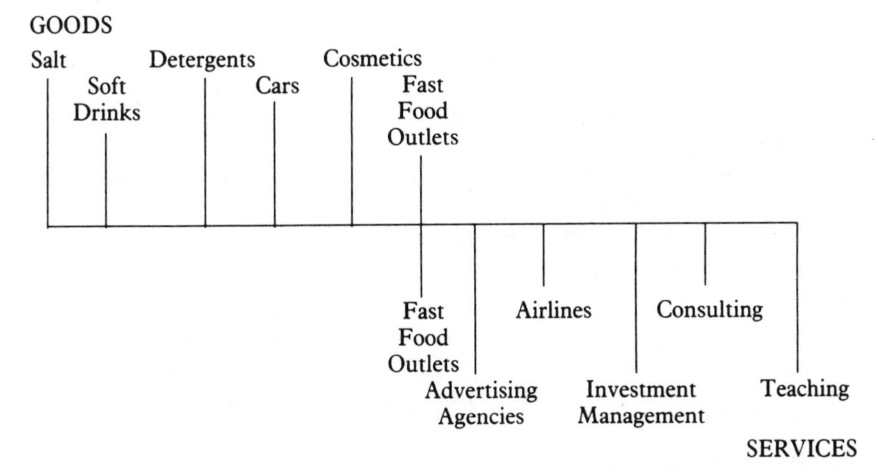

Figure 5.1. A goods–services continuum
Source: Shostack, G. L. 'Breaking Free from Product Marketing'

The continuum runs from goods that have almost no service characteristics to those that are almost purely service. The different parts of the continuum will require different types of management and marketing.

The development of the service society is part of the search for new pleasures and experiences. What were once luxury goods have become commonplace, and as they have become widely available, so they have ceased to create excitement and pleasure, and yield only comfort. As Herzberg would put it, they can satisfy us but they cannot motivate us. The search for the new is endless for in the process of gaining an experience we destroy its stimulating newness. The new products of the future will contain an increasing service element, for as material goods become more complex so they need various forms of service support for example technical advice.

The distinction between goods and services is largely arbitrary. If the reason for purchase and consumption is to gain benefits then we must examine both material and non-material goods for the benefits that they provide. We do not buy cars to possess large amounts of metal, or houses because we like bricks and mortar, but for the benefits, perhaps even the symbolic benefits, they provide. The more complex a society, and the more complex the ways that we use and experience products, the less valuable are product classifications. As Moran says:

> . . . In our complex service society there are no more product classes – not in a meaningful sense, only as figments of the file clerk's imagination . . .

> To some degree, in some circumstances, almost anything can be a substitute for almost anything else. A fifteen-cent stamp substitutes to some extent for an airline ticket.

Static classifications, even between goods and services, are unlikely to be satisfactory for the manager in planning a marketing campaign, for any realistic classification is a set of concepts rather than a description of the world as it is. The key in the analysis of service is to determine what is the core product or benefit and which characteristics of the service produce that benefit. The core product is the essential benefit provided by the service and the most useful categorisation of service products is one based upon the nature of the benefit. For example one can distinguish:

- ▽ Services that add value to or protect my physical possessions, such as police or fire services.
- ▽ Services that contribute to the physical well-being of the individual, for example leisure.
- ▽ Services that contribute to the emotional well-being of the individual, for example counselling.
- ▽ Services that contribute to the intellectual and moral well-being of the individual, for example education.

The way that a service is managed and marketed will depend on the sort of benefit that it provides, and the sort of relationship that is therefore created between producer and user. Focussing on the benefit provided by a product forces the organisation to think about the service from the user's point of view.

Service dimensions

Services can be distinguished from material goods along a number of dimensions.

Services	**Material Goods**
Intangible	Tangible
Cannot be stored	Storable
Cannot be owned	Can be owned
Difficult to standardise	Normally standardised
Production involves consumer	Production independent of consumer
Quality difficult to guarantee	Quality can be built into product
Does not persist through time	Persists through time

Services are difficult to grasp intellectually and difficult to monitor in practice, so much so that in the extreme it may be difficult to know whether one has actually had the service or not. If we get poor legal or financial advice it is possible to argue that we have not actually had the promised service. Even the case of very simple services such as cleaning it may be difficult to know whether they have been delivered without actually standing over people while they do the work. People are often willing to pay a high price for a service partly because this provides more of a guarantee that it will actually be delivered. High price provides a signal that the service can be trusted, not least because the supplier will want to protect future reputation. In providing services local authorities need to think how it is that people know that they have had a service. It is easy for the services provided by the local authority to be anonymous. To some extent the service manager must provide evidence that the service has been provided. This evidence may take a variety of forms. In education certificates provide evidence. Customised vehicles can provide evidence of services, as can making the service provider more visible through the wearing of uniforms or name-tags. In other cases the evidence that the service has been provided may come in the form of promotion and information.

The non-material character of services means that they cannot be stored or owned. In the case of manufactured goods, organisations can store the finished product — hold inventories — to meet fluctuations in demand. Service providers often work the other way round, storing the customer, not the service, in the form of queues or waiting lists. The service is often so organised for the benefit of the producer not the consumer or user. If queuing and waiting lists are unavoidable then the organisation should recognise the fact and create an environment in which waiting is not too unpleasant, or ensure that those on waiting lists are provided with good up-to-date information on their position. It is often not the waiting that is the cause of frustration and unhappiness but the uncertainty that accompanies it. The lack of inventories for services leads to famine or feast. The availability of a service will partly depend on how many other people want to use it, but it will tend to be the case that people will want to use services at the same time. It is also difficult to expand or contract service production to reflect demand. Even if it is possible to expand by hiring more staff it may take a great deal of time to do so. Good services are, therefore, inherently likely to generate demand that cannot be met. The service provider may face the marketing problem of how to control and limit demand rather than increase it.

When we buy or receive services we do not then own them, and the purchase does not involve a transfer of ownership, as it normally does with manufactured goods. Only the very rich can have exclusive possession of the services upon which they depend, such as medical, legal or accountancy services. The whole notion of property rights is difficult to maintain for services. Producers cannot easily assert their rights through patents, for it is difficult to describe and specify the detail of the service relationship. Purchasers do not retain continuing control of the service. When I purchase manufactured goods, I can take them home. I can choose the times at which I use them, and I can sell them again if I have finished with them or if I am dissatisfied. I can take them back and exchange them if they do not work. In the extreme, it may be that one can own services by owning the people that produce them through slavery or indenture. In ancient societies professionals such as doctors were sometimes slaves. Modern attempts to own the intangible service through owning those who provide it include binding employment practices that impose heavy sanctions on movement through loss of pension rights or perks, and the development of tightly specified systems that can be franchised, for example McDonald's and other fast-food franchises. But there are limits to these practices which make ownership and control difficult. The provision of a good service often makes demands upon individual skills and abilities, but the reputation that individuals thereby acquires makes them highly mobile and difficult to tie to the organisation. Material goods change what people possess, but services change what people are.

It is difficult to standardise the intangible, especially where it involves human behaviour that can change with mood and circumstances. The production line and the development of interchangeable parts allowed standardisation of industrial products and processes. New technology has allowed the standardisation of some service products, for example through the development of sophisticated booking systems for theatres or airlines, or in aspects of banking. But it is difficult to mechanise many processes, especially where they involve personal care and commitment. McDonalds do lay down a behavioural code, specifying such things as eye contact, and scripts are sometimes provided, for example for tour guides in Disneyland, but much of the service process is, in the nature of things, indeterminate. It may involve intimate relationships, as in the case of health services, social services or counselling work. Levitt's argument, that the efficient way of delivering services in the future will be through the use of high technology is, at best, a partial answer, for it ignores the extent to which people themselves form part of the service. The relationship that the client has with the doctor, social worker or teacher is part of the service that she or he receives. It can have a permanent effect on the way those who receive services see themselves.

Because those who deliver services must respond to circumstances, we rely upon professional skill and training and the standardisation of people's skills, rather than products and processes, to ensure quality. For manufactured products the nature of the product that is produced can be so specified that it can be built into a machine, leaving the operative very little discretion in the final outcome. It is inherent in the intangible and necessarily responsive nature of services that the product cannot be so specified. Quality in the service sector will always be difficult to assess, and will involve judgement. It will always be possible for people to debate whether the service that is provided by doctors, teachers or social workers is of high quality or not. Often people will, quite justifiably, be working with quite different criteria in evaluating a service. Much of the promotion work in a service industry will be concerned with the development of agreed standards both within the organisation and amongst those who receive its services. In the production of material goods standards can be specified and monitored: it may be difficult or impossible to do so for services.

The relationship between consumer and producer is more immediate and intricate in service production than in manufacturing industries. Since it is difficult to store services, producer and consumer may need to be present if it is to be delivered. The consumer is part of the production process. Producers or professionals cannot produce a good service on their own but need cooperation and involvement of the user. This is more true in some cases than others. We can distinguish between servicing people and servicing things; the more the person is involved in the service, the more necessary it is for the person to be present. Less personal services, such as financial services, can be provided at a distance, but for counselling, care or education, the consumer is part of the process.

User involvement in service production

Type of service	Degree of user involvement
Ancillary services	Low
Financial services	Low/medium
Care services	Medium
Educational services	High
Counselling services	High

The involvement of the consumer contributes to the difficulty of specifying quality, since the producer alone cannot determine, or assess, the quality of the experience. The way that the consumer behaves will partly determine the quality of the service. Subjective indicators of performance are inevitable, because quality is largely subjective. The subjective evaluation is not simply a result of the fact that objective measures are unavailable or hard to develop, but are of the very essence of the service experience. The danger is that a good customer or user comes to be seen as one who fits in with the producer's idea of how the service should be provided.

The management of the delivery of services will involve the management of the service users and the experience that they have. Managing services is more difficult than managing manufacturing production because the management process is not wholly internal to the organisation. The service organisation is necessarily an open system and the manager must not only manage the organisation but also its relation to the outside world.

Goods are produced: services are performed. The performance involves a relationship between producer and consumer that is often intimate and personal. The process of producing, selling and consuming goods can be spread through space and time. The production of services often cannot. Goods can be produced in factories, sold through wholesale or retail outlets and consumed in the privacy of one's own home. With services, all three processes take place at the same time and in the same place. There are no separate channels of distribution. The producer of goods is little interested in the circumstances in which people will consume them: the producer of services cannot avoid such a concern, for the circumstances of consumption are those of production.

The intimacy of the relationship between the producer and the consumer makes services much more involving than goods. I do not care, apart from generalised feelings of altruism, whether the person who made the pen I am writing with was happy or unhappy when they did so. It makes little difference to the pen and what I do with the pen makes little difference to them. The mood and feelings of the doctor, teacher, social worker or nurse, by contrast, can affect the service that I receive strongly and immediately. Equally my mood and feelings can affect the quality of the service. The production and consumption of services is not an anonymous process. The consequence is that marketing cannot take place wholly separately from the process of production and consumption, but, as I shall argue later must take place alongside it.

The service interaction

Services are social experiences, which are often much more bound up with our deepest feelings and understandings than are the goods with which we surround ourselves. Goods are often given symbolic meanings that go beyond their individual purposes, but with services the symbolic level is much more immediately apparent. Services involve relationships that are a necessary part of the service experience. The intimacy of the service exchange is difficult to establish and maintain. In many cases rapport must be established and judgements made very quickly, within the first few moments of the process of interaction beginning. There are dangers of stereotyping, for our judgements of those who are not like us are often poor. It is easy for behaviour to be mismatched. In order to understand others we need to know about the:

- ▽ Rules by which people operate in different situations.
- ▽ The language that people use and what they mean by what they say.
- ▽ Social customs of different groups.
- ▽ The assumptions with which people operate in different situations.
- ▽ The different roles that people are likely to play.

Without an understanding of the way that other groups and cultures operate we will fail to communicate effectively. Communication across cultures is very difficult since the same behaviour can have quite different meanings for different groups. Without such understandings the consumer marketing of services will not be effective. The processes to be understood in the case of service provision are much more difficult than in the case of the manufacturing industry because people are much more intimately involved.

Stereotyping is a means of avoiding involvement for those who are in constant contact with different people, such as doctors, teachers, social workers, or receptionists. It limits the commitment that we much make, and is usually done on the basis of single highly visible characteristics. Stereotyping allows the reduction of individual circumstances and cases to single categories — such as deserving and undeserving — at the expense of the receiver of the service. Stereotyping reduces the complex relationship of the service process to a single, probably inappropriate dimension. It is less likely the more the person providing the service is committed to the service role that they perform and the more that role forms part of their own conception of themselves. The value of professionalism lies largely in the identification of person and role, and a consequent reduction in the likelihood of stereotyping.

Services are social processes, produced, more like social dramas, not made like physical goods. Many of the analogies with the theatre hold, indeed some companies consciously use theatrical language, as in Disneyworld with its talk of roles, scripts and on- and off-stage. It is easy to see the functions performed by service providers as roles, but they are roles, as we shall see, peculiarly subject to conflict and ambiguity. The customer or consumer is frequently unaware of the script and the part that they must play in the service process. A major task in the service process is to manage the consumer and that means helping them to be aware of the script and the role they are playing. In service marketing a component of the management role must be to enable the consumer to play his or her part effectively.

Managing the consumer

Approaches to managing the consumer may be seen as negative or positive. Negative approaches are those that exclude the user from any control of the service process or in which their interests are systematically denied. Erving Goffman has described the way that 'total institutions' control the whole life of and personality of inhabitants, using a variety of dehumanising methods. Such extreme examples of control are found only in coercive institutions such as prisons, and perhaps on some occasions residential establishments. But there is always a danger of a resort to coercion and negative involvement, symbolised in the brutal architecture with which we disfigured some of our cities in the 1960s and 1970s. In such extreme cases control has replaced service altogether. The less power the service user has the greater the danger that the approach to his or her involvement will become negative.

A second negative approach is to exclude through restricting access. This may be done actively, through setting up barriers to the use of service, for example organisational gatekeepers who prevent people from getting a service. An extreme example is the gatekeepers on the doors of exclusive New York clubs and discotheques who keep out anyone who they do not think is interesting. Less active methods of exclusion may simply involve not letting people know that a service is available, an approach commonly used in social security. Dominance and incorporation may be used to control the consumer. Dominance involves excluding the user from any say in the nature of the service on the grounds that the provider knows best. Incorporation means involving representatives of the user on the provider's terms. Local leaders may be taken into the confidence of the organisation to manage a recalcitrant community, and to persuade people of the organisation's beliefs and interests.

Positive approaches to managing the consumer involve responsiveness and active involvement. The 'closeness to the customer' argument developed by Peters and Waterman in their book *In Search of Excellence* and taken up by a host of subsequent writers, has led to much greater recognition of the virtues of positive management of the consumer. As Peters and Waterman say:

> The good news from excellent companies is the extent to which, and the intensity with which the customers intrude into every nook and cranny of the business – sales, manufacturing, research and accounting. A simple message pervades the atmosphere. All business success rests on something labelled a sale, which at least momentarily weds company and customer. A simply summary of what our research uncovered on the customer is this: the excellent companies really are close to their customers. that's it. Other companies talk about it; the excellent companies do it.

The relationship between customer and provider, the 'wedding' to which Peters and Waterman refer must be that much closer in the case of services. Being close to the customer entails:

▽ An obsession with service.
▽ An obsession with quality.
▽ Finding a niche where you can do things better than others.
▽ Being oriented to value rather than cost.
▽ Listening to the customer.
▽ Understanding the customer.

In a service organisation where the product is essentially ephemeral, it is even more important to manage the consumer's experience and to help them through the system. The system has normally been designed by and for the professionals. It may suit them but not the service user. Those designing service systems need to think about:

▽ How the service user will experience them.
▽ The circumstances in which they will be used.
▽ How service users will feel when they come into the system.
▽ Where the system is likely to fail.

Marketing writers have argued that a number of elements must be added to the marketing mix when we are dealing with services. Normann talks of the core service and the peripherals. Others talk of the tangible clues, the augmented product, or the physical evidence. The point is that the more tangible is the product that we are delivering, the more we need to focus upon the physical evidence that it exists and that it has been delivered. With material goods the physical character can be taken for granted and our concern will be to create an image, and to ensure that it persists over time. The simpler the product, the more that one is concerned to create a persisting image. The advertising of a product such as Coca-Cola, Bisto gravy or Mars Bars, is simple image presentation, and has stayed constant for years, as with the Mars slogan 'A Mars a day helps you work, rest and play'. Change, as Coca-Cola found when it introduced the new Coke, can be dangerous.

The service encounter and the service product need symbols if they are to be real for us. Many of us, when we visit the doctor, are happy to get a prescription that shows something was wrong and that something has been done to solve the problem. When travelling by plane, we guard the ticket closely, as the physical evidence of the service. The nature of the physical evidence needs to represent the service and its value, so we expect airline tickets to be bigger than bus tickets, and we do not expect good lawyers to be housed in poor offices. Psychologists have studied the effect of the physical environment on the way that people feel and behave — the effect of colour, heat and so forth. There are well-established relationships between such factors as heat and aggression. They physical layout of offices will influence the way in which people are able to interact. We may well send confusing messages to people by, for example, avowing a caring image in shoddy and unwelcoming surroundings. It will be the physical aspects of a service that will allow us to make sense of it. We expect the physical signs to be in tune with the nature of service, and incongruity can make us uncertain and uncomfortable. We do not expect churches to be like airports, or schools like factories, and when they are we are uncertain how to behave.

The intricate involvement of provider and consumer in service industries means that the people in the organisation are crucial to quality. They are likely to have to fulfil multiple roles, for example both as producers and sales people for the organisation. For many services, especially those involving our bodies or our personalities, interaction with others is a *fundamental* part of the process. The skills, abilities, attitudes and behaviour of service deliverers will be crucial, the more important and intimate the service. The importance of those who actually delivery the service means that the distinction between the front-line — those who deliver the service — and the back-line — those who support them — is crucial. The importance of people means that they must be clear on what the organisation is trying to do, and this, in turn, means that the organisation must market to its employees to be sure that they know what the organisation's objectives are.

The process of production of services is much more fragmented than the production of goods. It is a series of individual events. The process of production is part of the service. I may not care much how the car I drive was produced. But I cannot but care about the process by which I am educated, nursed or housed. This is especially so where the process involves a continuing relationship as in caring or educational services. Employee discretion will play a large part in the process of producing many services. Both continuity, to ensure that the core service is delivered, and variation, to cope with the specific needs of individual consumers, and with changed circumstances, are needed in service systems.

The market mix for services is more complex than for goods. There are more variables to be considered and they interrelate strongly with one another. Developing a clear marketing mix strategy for services is also difficult because of the nature of the organisation. In a service organisation there is much less control of the service production and delivery process than in most manufacturing organisations, because the organisation is 'inside-out'.

Organisations tend to protect those elements of their operations that are most important. They will hold stocks in order to be able to ensure production in the face of shortage of materials. They will integrate backwards or forwards, so as to ensure control of key processes. They will make sure that there is organisational slack, to ensure that they have the capacity to deal with any unforeseen events or problems. In most organisations the production process will have a high priority and will be protected from external impacts. Senior managers, marketing and finance departments and others, will buffer production from external pressure. In the service organisation things are different, because production is done at the edge, not in the centre, of the organisation. The service organisation is inside-out, with production done in direct contact with the consumer. Staff are torn between representing the organisation and the client, causing role conflict and ambiguity.

It is more difficult in these circumstances to define the core product and to say who has the responsibility of guarding it. But if those who actually produce the service are to be protected from unwarranted buffeting, it is necessary to determine what is essential and what is not. This entails understanding the whole service system. Shostack has proposed a method of 'service blueprints', essentially the application of work analysis techniques to service processes, in order to be able to determine core elements. Whatever method is used, organisations need to determine the core service in order to be able to protect it, otherwise they may find themselves protecting the less essential inside of the organisation, by subjecting the productive surface to pressure and uncertainty.

Conclusion

The differences between services and material goods, and the differences in management that are appropriate are only beginning to be recognised. Much of the innovation in manufacturing over the last twenty years has centred in systems, not products or techniques. Market dominance has derived from new ways of producing, based upon 'flexible specialisation'. New technology has enabled firms to gain the advantages of economies of scale and scope from short production runs, responding rapidly to changes in demand. Organisations have focused upon the whole process, from purchase of materials and labour and inventory procedures, to delivery of the product, as a single system. New means of organising, such as sub-contracting and franchising have developed, reflecting the importance of control of systems, rather than ownership of plant. The world-wide spread of MacDonald's illustrates the commercial success of system-based control.

Services are now subject to the pressure to analyse the whole system of service production and delivery. This pressure has three implications for the analysis of the role of marketing in the public services. First, we must analyse marketing as part of the total system of design, production and delivery. Second, we need to consider how the various parts of the organisation add value to and create the final product. Finally, we need to see how one part of the organisation relates to another in the total process. Each of these themes will be taken up in the following chapters on local government.

Questions and Exercises

▲ 1. *What kind of service do you provide? Does it:*
Add value to or protect people's property?
Contribute to people's physical well-being?
Contribute to people's mental well-being?
Contribute to people's intellectual or moral development?

▲ 2. *Consider a service which you provide or in which you have an interest. Is it high or low on the following characteristics of a service?*

	High	*Low*
Tangibility		
Storability		
Capable of being owned		
Standardisable		
Involvement of consumer in production		
Quality capable of being guaranteed		
Persists through time		

▲ 3. *What evidence will people have that they have had your service if they have done so?*

▲ 4. *How will:*
Service user experience your service?
In what circumstances will the service be used?
How will those who use your service be feeling when they use it?
When is the service likely to fail?

▲ 5. *How would you describe the service interaction involved in:*
Education?
Social services?
Environmental health?
Housing?

▲ 6. *How is the consumer managed in the service system with which you are familiar?*

6 The local authority and its services

Key points

▲ *The market segments for the authority as a whole determined by:*
 ▽ *The social characteristics of the area*
 ▽ *Interest groups in the community.*
 ▽ *Those to whom the authority is accountable.*
 ▽ *Corporate responsibilities.*

▲ *The need for the local authority to develop a clear position and the tensions involved.*

▲ *The responsibility of the authority to develop and promote the local area.*

▲ *The importance of a pricing strategy for the authority.*

▲ *The relationship between the authority and the consumer:*
 ▽ *Planning and designing services.*
 ▽ *Delivering services.*
 ▽ *Evaluating services.*

▲ *Complaints and the role of the authority in empowering the consumer.*

The local authority needs to market both itself and its services. the greatest part of an authority's activities are concerned with the delivery of individual services. But the local authority is more than the service that it delivers. It must have a care for the whole of the local community and area, and must act as an advocate in the present and a guardian for the future. It is constituted for local government, which involves the process of collective choice between competing alternative uses of resources, and has a responsibility for developing a vision of the community. Marketing can play a role in the development of direction and vision. In this chapter the concepts of market segmentation, market position and marketing mix are analysed to see how they can be used to develop vision and purpose.

The markets of the local authority

Market segmentation — the division of the market into relevant parts — is a key component of the marketing analysis. Individual services will have their consumers/clients/users, but the authority will also need to consider who it is serving. The authority itself will face different segments that can be analysed along a number of dimensions:

▽ The social characteristics of the local community.
▽ The interest groups in the local community.
▽ Those to whom the authority must be accountable.
▽ The corporate responsibilities of the authority.

Segmentation on the basis of the characteristics of the local community involves detailed analysis of the nature of the local social structure. The complexity of local communities has changed greatly in recent years. We are a multi-cultural society. In major cities, in particular, people come from a wide range of cultural backgrounds, and have many different lifestyles. This range of cultures is not new but goes back many centuries, for example in ports such as Liverpool. It involves people who have come from different parts of the British Isles as well as from other countries. Local authorities need to know a great deal more about cultures and life-styles if they are to design services that meet varying needs. The range of cultures, and the demands that they impose, is strikingly illustrated by the number of languages, more than a hundred, spoken by children in schools in the Inner London Education Authority. But all authorities face the need to consider the way that the needs of the various communities that they serve can best be met.

Social change and developing social attitudes have led to a recognition that the community must be seen as varying along a number of dimensions. It will contain geographic segments, which are still strong, particularly in rural areas. The reorganisation of 1974 changed names, but often left loyalties intact. The county of Hereford and Worcester still contains two different communities: the people of Sutton Coldfield still want to retain their independence from Birmingham. In many authorities facilities and services are still decided on the basis of ensuring fair shares for each of the pre-existing communities, sometimes leading to duplication and overlap. Geography is still an important factor and a sense of place an important part of community loyalty and identity.

The recognition of the role of the local authority in promoting equal opportunities provides a further basis of segmentation. The local authority has a duty under the Race Relations Act 1976 to work for the elimination of racial discrimination. the needs of women are being recognised by many authorities as a corporate matter for the authority as whole. Authorities are increasingly coming to recognise that the needs of people with disabilities are the responsibility of the authority as a whole and not only of the social services or education departments. Segmentation on the basis of the opportunity available on different social groups needs to be part of the general strategy of the authority.

The local community may also be divided on the basis of need. Different circumstances create different levels of need. It may be that our concepts of the appropriate form for local services is based upon a pattern of organisation that no longer pertains. Much of the welfare state was based upon the notion of the nuclear family and may not be appropriate to a world with high levels of marital breakdown and a large and increasing number of one-parent families. The nature of need will change as social circumstances change. Other segments based on need might be young children, the frail elderly or the mentally-ill, all of whom will have needs that go beyond the individual services of the authority. Some local authorities have been using segmental analysis, for example to:

▽ Consider the library and leisure needs of the elderly.
▽ Analyse the access problems of people with disabilities.
▽ To analyse the travel needs of the disabled.
▽ To determine the leisure needs of the young.
▽ To consider the problems that one parent families have in the use of services.
▽ To consider the security needs of the elderly.

Interest segmentation is based upon the notion that many people will be organised into specific groups which express a whole range of types of interest. In any authority there will be a large number of such groups. The lines of division may be based upon service use, for example in the case of tenants' associations or parent groups. There will also be interest groups concerned with the environment or sport. There will be general interest groups concerned to promote the interests of business and industry, or to represent the interests of trade unionists. Voluntary organisations will pursue the interests of specific social groups. Building and maintaining links with such groups will be the responsibility of the authority as a whole. The networking role of the local authority involves a strong element of marketing with the authority trying to influence the needs of the local area through its influence with other bodies.

An important aspect of segmentation for the authority as a whole is to consider the various segments to which it must be accountable. The authority must think about who are the stakeholders in its activities. The authority does not account for its activities only through the ballot box. The election is the foundation of the legitimacy of the authority, but it is not the only way that legitimacy is created. Local authorities, under the Rates Act 1984, must consult bodies which are seen to be representative of non-domestic ratepayers in their area about expenditure and rating policy. Authorities are also, in practice, called to account for many of their actions by central government and the courts. The recognition of the need for wider accountability has led a number of authorities to establish forums in which community groups are represented. The process of accountability can be an opportunity for marketing and for the authority to build its image.

It is the responsibility of the authority to ensure that the organisation is not segmented along purely departmental lines. The authority must have a care for the community as a whole. This need has been increasingly recognised since the 1970s and sophisticated strategic planning and management processes have been developed by many authorities. In one shire district detailed statistical analysis was used to identify the problems arising from recession and unemployment and key client groups were identified as the basis of the authority's strategy which was expressed as being:

- ▽ To identify and respond to those in need.
- ▽ To move from the distinction between corporate and service priorities to a single set of Council priorities.
- ▽ To enable council policies and initiatives to become more responsive to rapidly changing circumstances.
- ▽ To focus existing services more explicitly on the wider issues and problems facing the district.
- ▽ To create a framework for improved co-ordination in dealing with these issues.
- ▽ To provide a basis for improving the way in which the authority works with many other agencies who have a crucial role to play in responding to these issues.

The development of an authority's strategy depends upon an initial analysis of the segments that make up its complex and changing environment. This analysis is a task for the authority as a whole and not for the individual departments which make it up.

It is part of the role of the authority to consider how the different services that it provides relate to the various community segments that it must serve and to the authority's overall strategy. A number of authorities have developed this sort of analysis determining the interrelationship between client groups and service. It is possible to ask, for each service that the authority provides:

- ▽ What contribution is a particular service making to the needs of a particular client groups?
- ▽ What contribution is the service making to the authority's overall strategy?

Market position

Market position is the stance that the authority takes towards its market — the relation between the producer and the consumer. It is a mixture of image and purpose, as expressed in the core values of the authority. Our image of the authority will be influenced by the way that it expresses itself. Some authorities use slogans to express their image and position. Examples include:

- ▽ Braintree means business
- ▽ Services well worth defending: well worth fighting for.
- ▽ Working with the community.
- ▽ Your council — building a future.
- ▽ Socialism at work.
- ▽ People and services first.
- ▽ Serving the community – meeting the need.
- ▽ The pace setter.
- ▽ Aiming for excellence.
- ▽ Serving the community.

Such slogans may serve more than a promotional purpose if they encapsulate key values. They may backfire if they express an aim that cannot be fulfilled. Saying that people and services come first will ring hollow if people feel that they come a poor second to the authority's own staff.

General slogans need to be carried through into statements of the way that organisation works. Braintree elaborates its slogan in the following core values:

- ▽ We are customer orientated.
- ▽ We believe in the ability of individuals.
- ▽ We must be responsive and responsible.
- ▽ We believe in quality.
- ▽ We are action oriented.

Such statements of value can be used to develop detailed action plans as Braintree has done. Value statements need to be clear and simple, and to tell the public what it can expect from the authority, and staff what services they are supposed to deliver and how they are supposed to deliver them.

An important aspect of the market position of the authority can be expressed in the tension between caring and efficiency; some authorities will lay more emphasis on the value of caring others on efficiency. It may be that both are equally possible. Paul Beresford, the Leader of Wandsworth claims:

> Conservative Wandsworth Council has proved that it is possible, by using ordinary common sense, to produce high quality services at relatively low cost.

But there will always be a tension between cost and caring and the position of authorities will vary. The overall aspect of this tension is a matter for the authority as a whole to resolve.

Local authorities will also vary in their position in taking either a narrow or a wide view of their responsibilities. Some authorities will take a general position, seeing it as their responsibility to contribute to the whole development of the local area, others will focus more narrowly on service. Many authorities that have been strongly affected by unemployment have taken a very wide view of their responsibilities. The increasing complexity of the problems faced by local authorities is tending to force them to take a wider view of their responsibilities. The wider the role of the authority the more the authority as a whole must develop a clear strategic perspective on the relationship between services.

Working out the position of the authority may involve conflicts. Providing a better quality of service may lead the authority into conflict with staff who may be adversely affected by the demands that better service makes. The statement of a position is not simply the use of slogans or logos, but deciding where the authority lies along key strategic dimensions. The dimensions that need to be considered are:

Key strategic dimensions in local authority positioning

Cost	v.	Caring
General	v.	Specific
Reactive	v.	Proactive
Centralised	v.	Decentralised
Corporate	v.	Departmental
Efficiency	v.	Effectiveness

Where the authority stands on dimensions such as these will determine the authorities position and therefore its marketing strategy.

The authority's marketing mix

The marketing mix is the decisions on the set of variables — product, price, promotion and place — that the authority can vary to produce different marketing strategies. Most of the decisions on the marketing mix will relate to individual services but there are some aspects of the decisions that fall to the authority as a whole. Most of the individual services produced by local authorities are based on statutory duties, but the authority also has two generalised roles that go beyond the provision of individual services:

- ▽ Developing the local area.
- ▽ Developing corporate services.

The authority may wish to promote the local area as a centre for tourism or economic development. The authority also has duty to protect the local area, for example by mounting campaigns as a number of local authorities recently did against NIREX plans to bury nuclear waste in the locality. The physical integrity of the area is part of the authority's responsibilities.

Local authorities are increasingly involved with outside agencies — with health authorities, water authorities, voluntary agencies, central government and the private sector. The local authority has a strong role to play in considering how its activities link with those of other agencies and how effective local networks can be created. The authority can have a direct influence on the output of other agencies, not least because they are frequently represented on these bodies or involved in funding them. One authority, for example, found that four out of five of its members represented the authority on outside bodies and in one year attended up to 100 meetings. Such representation provides a marketing opportunity for the authority, and a process was established for ensuring that members were well serviced in their work on outside bodies.

The authority may market itself as a :

▽ Tourist area.
▽ Centre for industrial development.
▽ Centre for the development of service industries.
▽ Shopping centre.
▽ Commercial centre.

The authority may market itself to:

▽ Central government.
▽ The private sector.
▽ Overseas.
▽ The voluntary sector.

The introduction of the single market in 1992 will require authorities to consider the implications for them. Already many authorities have been active in the European Economic Community which may be an important source of finance. Such marketing of the authority will involve resolving tensions such as that between preserving the character of the area and attracting people to it, and that is a role for the authority as a whole.

Local government in general and individual authorities in particular have had a bad press, particularly at the national level. But changes in the news media have created opportunities for influence:

▽ Local radio has grown in significance.
▽ The development of free newspapers, often needing copy, has provided a medium in which stories can be placed.
▽ Some local authorities have developed their own newspapers and newssheets.

Local government is fast realising the importance of promotion in giving itself an appropriate image both locally and nationally, and perhaps even internationally, and in attracting money and jobs to the local area. The increasing pressure on local authorities from the centre makes the development of a clear promotions strategy important. Without the support that good promotion may help to develop local authorities will be increasingly vulnerable.

Local authorities have been recognising the importance of promotion. A 1985 survey found that 112 shire districts employed public relations specialists and had budgets ranging from £25000 to £1 million while most large authorities have a public relations function. Public relations is an aspect of management that does need central co-ordination in the authority. It is not likely that each department will be large enough to deal with its own public relations in a skilful way. The importance of public relations can be illustrated by the case of Strathclyde Regional Council. In 1986/7 they produced 835 press releases which resulted in 35000 column inches of newspaper coverage. Other coverage of the council resulted in another 25000 column inches of coverage. Strathclyde, given its size and importance within the Scottish system of government, is perhaps unusual but the role of public relations in local authorities is important and is often underemphasised.

The image of the authority will be expressed visually as well as in statements of values and mission. At the extreme, visual images can take on an iconic significance, with a single image embodying a whole set of values and beliefs. Such iconic symbols are most strongly developed in religious systems. Representations of the Madonna and Child or of the Cross imply a whole body of thought and belief in a condensed and accessible form. It is often impossible to explain in other ways that is represented by a visual image. Words written and spoken do not carry the same power and simplicity. The authority needs to consider carefully the visual image that it presents to the public.

The visual image that people have of the authority will be formed both in the particular and the general.

- ▽ Logos can give identity.
- ▽ Uniforms may create an images of efficiency and give the workforce a clear sense of identity. A number of local authorities are putting their staff into uniforms of various sorts.
- ▽ The publications of the authority will create an image.
- ▽ The communications of the authority — its letters or its bills — will create a visual image.
- ▽ The offices and other buildings of the authority will contribute to the picture that people have of it.

Visible images will be formed by the architecture and physical layout of the town hall. The great, nineteenth century town halls may create a feeling of dignity and solidity but they may also intimidate people. They express a position of dominance and paternalism which many authorities want to replace with one of service and responsiveness.

Authorities need a clear promotions strategy that is based upon a clear corporate image and identity. Without such a strategy there is likely to be a poor view of the authority both in the local community and among its own staff. A consistent finding of surveys has been that there is much ignorance about local government. The Widdicombe research found that, though the general level of knowledge was quite high, there were still 48% of respondents to the survey who were 'not very well informed' or 'uninformed'. A promotions strategy can overcome this ignorance. Ignorance of its activities and apathy will leave the local authority vulnerable to the criticisms of central government and others.

The local authority's corporate promotion role also includes its duty to allow access to and provide information for the public. The statutory requirements to provide information have been growing, though other legislation is limiting the right of the authority to decide the form in which information is provided, through preventing political statements. The requirement for local authorities to provide information and the limitation of its freedom to decide on the form of publicity is in notable contrast to the closed and secretive nature of central government. The movement to greater freedom of information has not resulted only from legislation but also from initiatives by local authorities. Bradford City Council produced 'A Code of Practice about Public Access to Internal Documents' in 1984, which allowed wide access and encouraged officers to:

Write openly whenever you can. If possible, write your document so that it does not need to be restricted.

Local authorities must produce a range of public reports, notably the annual report on the authority's activities. Many of these excellent documents, though they might be more widely circulated by adopting a newspaper format as is done in some authorities. Many well produced reports are seen by very few people.

It would be a mistake simply to assume that people are anxious for more information about local government and local services. As one chief executive said in a survey on freedom of information:

I have not the slightest objection to giving (this) information to the public, the real problem is how do you get it over to the people who do not want to know and, really, I think, that is where the Government was wrong. They assumed that there was a mass of people just waiting, thirsting for information . . .

No doubt there is a great deal of truth in this. No doubt, also, it is equally true for manufacturing companies, or any other private sector organisation. The point is that people should get the information that they want or need, which is likely to be about things that are of direct concern to them, for example arrangements for school entrance or for refuse collection. For example, many authorities will not remove certain types of refuse but do not tell the householder what they will and will not collect. An information strategy is about ensuring the targeting of information.

Pricing

Local authorities need a clear pricing strategy. Local authority services are priced either indirectly through the rates and in future the community charge or directly through specific charges. The Green Paper, *Paying for Local Government*, details the extent of charging:

In 1984/5 income to local authorities' rate fund accounts from sales fees and charges amount in England to some £2600 million — equivalent to 60% of the yield from domestic rates. When income to the main local authority trading accounts and the housing revenue accounts is added, these figures are increased to £5250m and 115% respectively.

Charges are already made for more than 600 individual services. The extent to which local authorities are required to charge and the degree to which they will choose to charge for services are both likely to increase. Clearly the importance of income from charges requires an explicit strategy.

Some authorities have made detailed studies of their charging policies. Bovaird, in a study of Dudley's policy, says;

. . . it is necessary that the authority does consider and give clear guidance on its stance over the main issues relevant to a coherent authority wide charging policy. If this is not done, then there is inevitably a tendency for serious anomalies to creep into the range of charges made (and not made). When these become glaringly obvious, rapid reversals of policy tend to be made, which are not always well researched and can give an impression of erratic and arbitrary decision-making, which maximises the psychological resistance to the charges made.

The Cooper and Lybrand study (DoE) of pricing in local government found:

▽ There was not a systematic approach to pricing.
▽ Rules of thumb sometimes defined costs wrongly.
▽ 'Copy-cat' pricing is common.
▽ Bad reasons are used for less than full cost pricing.
▽ Few review their pricing policy regularly.

The report recommended that any review should consider the following questions.

▽ What is the purpose and intended client group of the service?
▽ Is a charge inherently inappropriate? If not, why not?
▽ What are the full costs of providing the service?
▽ Should the aim be to recover more than the full cost?
▽ What proportion of the full cost should be subsidised?
▽ Should the subsidy be flat-rate or variable?
▽ Should it be means tested?
▽ How does this subsidy rank among other priorities?

The Government has increased the range of charges that can be made by local authorities, for example in planning and education. The trend is towards more explicit charging for services. Local authorities also need a clear pricing policy in order to be able to trade with each other and with other organisations. Many services are provided by one authority for another, for example in social services or education. Local authorities have also been increasingly required to bid for specific grants or finance to central government or other bodies such as the Training Commission. The ability effectively to do so entails knowledge of unit costs and pushes authorities towards the pricing of their services.

The authority and the consumer

In the discussion of marketing I made the distinction between strategic marketing and consumer marketing. Consumer marketing will largely be the responsibility of the service departments. But the authority as a whole will also have a role to play in consumer aspects of the marketing process. Local authorities, spurred on by bodies such as the National Consumer Council and the Local Government Training Board, have given increasing attention to the relationship with those whom they serve. We may consider the relationship as having three stages:

▽ Planning and designing services.
▽ Delivering services.
▽ Evaluating services.

The relationship with the consumer is least developed in the service design and planning stage. The sort of process of product piloting and market testing that might be used in the private sector is much less developed in local authorities. Authorities might well use more experiments and small scale piloting. Potential users might be involved in the design of housing, schools and residential homes. More use might be made of surveys at the design and planning stage to determine priorities and need. Such surveys might be used as part of the process of designing service specifications in order to meet the requirements of the competitive tendering process. Consumers might also play a larger part in the delivery of many services for, as I have argued, the consumer is part of the production process in a service organisation. The passive relationship of the client to the professional is now being questioned not simply for reasons of power and rights but also because a service that gives inadequate attention to the role of the consumer is likely to be more inefficient.

It is, perhaps, in evaluating services that the role of the consumer is greatest. A number of local authorities have started to use market surveys as a means of determining consumer satisfaction. The development of reliable and valid instruments for consumer satisfaction is important for this purpose. Such surveys need to be continued over time, for it is the changes in satisfaction that are more valuable than the absolute levels. It may tell me relatively little that 80% of people are satisfied with a service, but a decline in satisfaction from 80% to 70% would be clear signal of possible problems. The work of Cleveland County Council in surveying over a long period of time has illustrated the relationships, often not obvious, between the level and quality of service and public perception. Consumer satisfaction surveys conducted over a period of years will provide authorities with a strong data base for the evaluation of their service standards.

Complaints can also play a major part in helping an authority to monitor and evaluate services as well as getting closer to the consumer. The local authority as a whole has a responsibility to ensure that the users of services have the means of gaining redress for service failures. In fact, local authorities pay little attention to complaints. A recent study found that few authorities had formal complaints procedures, and that, if they did, staff were often unaware of it:

> . . . only social services departments had special registers of complaints in a majority of authorities, while on the average only 20% of other service departments appeared to possess them.

Local authorities might make positive use of complaints, perhaps by actively creating the opportunity to complain, through office or cards on which complaints could be registered. Some authorities do this through the use of job tickets for housing repairs, which contain a section where tenants can state whether or not they were satisfied with the repairs.

Harlow District Council has developed a positive approach to complaints involving a number of clear stages. The approach has the following components.

- ▽ Standard written procedures for all departments.
- ▽ Staff fully trained and aware of responsibilities and procedures.
- ▽ Members aware of procedures and their part.
- ▽ Adequate information to the public about the authorities activities and problems to minimise complaints.
- ▽ Opportunity for the complainant to discuss or clarify complaints.
- ▽ Information on the role of the ombudsman where complainants remain dissatisfied.
- ▽ Contact points and information about complaints procedure and local ombudsman well publicise. (K. Madden "Handling Complaints in an Open Culture", *Local Government Chronicle* 5 August 1988).

Complaints can be more than simply an indication of where the authority has failed but also an indication of where remedial action may be needed and a means of quality control and assurance. The local authority has the responsibility to ensure that the voice of the consumer or user can be heard and that there is a system of representation and redress for those who use its services.

More generally the sort of things that the authority might review in examining its relationships with consumers include the following:

▽ Forms – ensuring that they are designed so that they can be easily understood and completed.
▽ Telephone – ensuring that people can get through to the right place in the authority, and that staff answer the phone in a friendly and helpful fashion. Some authorities have made great efforts to ensure that they develop telephone answering systems that try to ensure that callers are always responded to positively whoever they might come through to. Answering machines with emergency numbers may also be useful as may freephone systems in some cases.
▽ Letters – ensuring that they are written in a way that can be easily understood.
▽ Complaints – developing effective positive complaints procedures, and analysing the incidence of complaints in order to gain information on quality.
▽ Information – ensuring that the authority has effective means of providing information to consumers, for example through leaflets and newspapers.
▽ Campaigns – campaigns will be necessary to develop new approaches or services. In certain cases professionally organised campaigns may be needed.
▽ Corporate image – ensuring that the authority has the image that it wants and that it promotes its image effectively to the public.
▽ Accessibility – ensuring that the channels for service delivery are appropriate and effective, for example examining the value of decentralisation.

These issues can be monitored at the corporate level, and the development of effective systems will largely be a local authority responsibility.

Conclusion

The local authority needs a corporate marketing role, to ensure that there is an effective marketing strategy and an effective approach to relations with the consumer. It needs to ensure that an active approach is maintained towards the local community – for example through the use of regular surveys to canvass opinion. Richmond-on-Thames uses such surveys to monitor the effectiveness of services and to provide the basis of action to improve the quality of service. The greater part of the authority's role in marketing will be at the level of strategic marketing, rather than dealing with individual services. At a time of rapid change it will need to be concerned with the range of services and with the development of new services, for example economic development or the promotion of tourism. It will have a role in examining the overall strategy for the delivery and pricing of services. Most importantly it will need to devise an appropriate promotions strategy, to ensure good relations with the local community.

Questions and Exercises

▲ *1. Has your authority got an overall marketing strategy? Is so, what are its components?*

▲ *2. Where does your authority stand on the following dimensions that might be used to characterise its position.*

Cost	-------------------------	*Caring*
General	-------------------------	*Specific*
Reactive	-------------------------	*Proactive*
Centralised	-------------------------	*Decentralised*
Corporate	-------------------------	*Departmental*
Efficient	-------------------------	*Effective*

▲ *3. What dimensions would you use to describe the overall, position your authority takes towards those it serves?*

▲ *4. How might your authority promote the local area? As a:*

	Yes	*No*
Tourist area		
Shopping centre		
Centre for industrial development		
Centre for service development		
Commercial centre		
Other		

▲ *5. What tensions are there in your authority's image?*

▲ *6. What are the elements that would make up an effective promotions policy for your authority?*

7 Marketing and the service department

Key points

- ▲ *The wide range of services that are involved in each service department and the need for a differentiated strategy.*
- ▲ *The need to identify the consumer*
- ▲ *Distinguishing between the direct recipients of the service, those who benefit, directly or indirectly and those who are advocates.*
- ▲ *Positioning — identifying the distinctive difference of the service.*
- ▲ *The key dimensions of the service that is produced:*

  collective v. individual
  positive v. negative
  control v. support
  compulsory v. voluntary
  mandatory v. discretionary
- ▲ *The implications of pricing services.*
- ▲ *The determinants of the need for promotion of services.*
- ▲ *The difficulty of distributing local authority services.*

Most of the marketing that the local authority does will be concerned with individual services. Local authorities provide a huge range of services and each service department is itself a collection of different services. The local authority has much in common with the holding company dealing in a range of products that may be very unlike one another. Some types of authority are more varied than others — the London boroughs and the metropolitan districts came close to being all purpose authorities, while the shire districts have a relatively narrow range of functions. The major functions of shire districts and metropolitan districts are illustrated below:

Services in Shire and Metropolitan districts

Shire districts	*Metropolitan districts*
Museums and art galleries	Social Services
Housing	Education
Town and country planning	Libraries
Highways	Museums and art galleries
Environmental health	Housing
Environmental services	Town and country planning
Recreation	Highways
Tourism	Environmental services
Licensing	Environmental health

Registration	Recreation Tourism Licensing Registration

These are only the main functions of authorities under the broadest of headings; much more detailed categorisations are possible. The education service, for example, will provide a range of direct and ancillary services as illustrated below:

Education services

Direct services	*Ancillary services*
Nursery education	Meals and milk
Primary education	Medical inspection
Secondary education	Travelling facilities
Further education	Clothing
Adult education	
Higher education	
Special education	
Careers	
Youth and community	

More detailed categorisations are, of course, possible within these broad headings, for example further education can be divided into advanced and non-advanced education, vocational and non-vocational and many other groupings. An analysis of the product will entail a detailed analysis of the services provided at the point of delivery.

The range of goods and services provided by authorities requires a differentiated marketing strategy. Different approaches will be needed for different services and for different aspects of individual services. The first task is to decide which groups of people the department is providing services for — the market segmentation process. The local authority, as a collection of diverse services, provides a number of different service products to a number of different segments. Different services will adopt different approaches towards the people that they serve.

- ▽ Mass marketing — some will adopt a mass marketing approach producing one service for all segments, for example street lighting.
- ▽ Differentiated marketing — some will adopt differentiated approach producing different services for different segments, for example social services attempting to find different services to meet the needs of diverse groups such as vulnerable children, people with physical or mental handicaps or the elderly.
- ▽ Focused marketing — some will adopt a focused approach producing one service for one segment, for example secondary education.

Inappropriate matches between segments and products may lead to major problems for example some authorities now face major problems in housing because of adopting a mass marketing strategy of high rise blocks for what has become a highly differentiated market. A single type of housing or education will not meet increasingly diversified demand.

Who are the clients?

Service departments must consider who the actual and potential client groups for its services are. To some extent they are defined by statute:

- ▽ The Education Act 1944 requires local authorities to provide education for children between the ages of 5 and 16.
- ▽ The Chronically Sick and Disabled Persons Act 1970 requires the provision of services for people who have disabilities.
- ▽ The Control of Pollution Act 1974 defines the various client groups for refuse collection.

An individual department will serve a range of client groups. The education department will provide services for:

- ▽ Nursery children.
- ▽ Primary children.
- ▽ Secondary pupils.
- ▽ Pupils with special education needs.
- ▽ Further and higher education students.
- ▽ Young people.
- ▽ Adults.

Further categorisations are possible. The authority might analyse the services that it is providing for pupils from different cultural and ethnic backgrounds, or for boys and girls, or in specific geographical areas, or in terms of social and economic deprivation. Definitions of client groups may be difficult, and may change over time. In areas of high unemployment the age up to which individuals are considered to be 'youths' may be much higher than in other areas requiring a different form of youth service provision.

There will be multiple and overlapping categories that will need to be used to segment the market for a service. The local authority needs to take account of the specific needs of segments, not simply design a general or average service and attempt to modify it for specific client groups. To be treated as special, not requiring the 'normal' service, may carry elements of stigma. Segmentation is therefore important at the design stage and not only in the delivery of service.

Some departments provide services for all members of the public: the work of the environmental health officer or the engineer in controlling pollution or providing street lighting may benefit everybody. The service may be collectively consumed with no identifiable individual user. But even in such cases different groups may have different interests. Street-lighting policy and practice may have an influence on the extent of crimes of violence against women. Even for highly generalised services client groups may be identifiable. The danger of assuming that the client is the community as a whole is that the authority produces an average type of service without consulting groups with possibly different interests. Each service might benefit from analysing the benefits that it attempts to provide in terms of the impact on different client groups, for example:

- ▽ Children.
- ▽ Old people.
- ▽ Ethnic minorities.
- ▽ Women.

- ▽ The unemployed.
- ▽ Young people.
- ▽ Single parent families.
- ▽ Mothers with young children.
- ▽ People with disabilities.
- ▽ The homeless.

Many other categories might be relevant in particular authorities, for example people living in isolated communities in some shire counties.

Local authority services may also be analysed as having clients at different levels:

- ▽ There are those who actually receive the service.
- ▽ There are those who act on behalf of the direct recipients of services.
- ▽ There are those who benefit directly from the output of the service.
- ▽ There are those who benefit indirectly from the output of the service.

In the case of education the direct clients are the pupils or students in the authority's schools and colleges. They can be seen as the primary client. The secondary client, acting on behalf of pupils may be the parent or guardian. Local industry and commerce may be the direct beneficiaries of the output of the education service. The indirect beneficiary of education may be the public as a whole or specific groups such as publishers of educational books or equipment. Similar analyses can be carried out for other services. For example, in social services it is easy to see that the client has a number of layers and that there may be many hidden beneficiaries. Where secondary clients do not exist it may be valuable to invent them. We may provide advocates to speak on behalf of those who are not able to express their own interests adequately, as some authorities have done in developing advocacy for people with mental handicaps.

Local authorities should consider both positive and negative benefits in analysing the clients for its services. Many services will benefit some at the expense of harming others. The new road may help the driver, but destroy somebody else's home. Dog owners may enjoy using the park to exercise their dogs but possibly at the expense of ruining the pleasure of others. In order to be able to perform the necessary cost benefit analysis the negative as well as the positive benefits of services must be identified.

It is necessary to make an effort to discover the way that the prospective client will value the service which may change with experience. In the early stages of the provision of a service the emphasis may be upon quantity, but as provision develops the concern may shift to quality or variety. Services may be seen as having a life-cycle, and the way that they are experienced by users will vary at different stages in the cycle. At first they may provide satisfaction simply because they are new, but as that novelty wears off so more will come to be expected.

Authorities often lack the information necessary for segmentation analysis. In some cases change has led to authorities developing better client information systems. In education the impact of falling pupil rolls in the 1970s and 1980s has led authorities to develop much more accurate pupil forecasting systems. But in many cases there has been a lack of analysis of client segments simply because the information is not available. Social services is an obvious example. The government, following the Chronically Sick and Disabled Persons Act 1970, suggested that need might be determined by the use of local surveys, individual enquiries to each household, or bringing together information held by statutory and voluntary agencies. Many authorities found the process of gathering information too costly and have inadequate knowledge of need. Research suggests that less than a quarter of the elderly in need are actually reached by services.

The less the actual recipient of the service is identified, the more difficult it is to design a product that will actually satisfy the need or demand involved. The danger of designing for the anonymous average is that the average may be everybody's second choice. Services need to be designed not for the average but for particular groups and individuals. The danger of standardised approaches is that they do not match local circumstances and specific needs.

The process of analysing who the service is actually for may be creative in that the providers of a service may not simply look for customers who are 'out there', but may encourage the development of particular groups. Community work may serve to strengthen social relations and, effectively, create segments. Jeremy Seabrook in his study of Walsall's experiment in decentralisation, *The Idea of Neighbourhood*, describes the way that local workers acted to generate community groups. As an organ of government, the local authority has a duty to help structure and create local organisations. As Normann says, in his study of service management:

> Market segmentation should be conceived not only from the point of view of the 'needs' of the consumer, but also in terms of his willingness to participate and his participation style.

The authority needs to create knowledgeable service users. Glasgow and a number of other authorities, for example, have attempted to develop active self-supporting tenants in the housing service. The decline in resources relative to need that has followed from the cutback in local expenditure means that services must engage in more sophisticated analysis of segments and position. It is not possible to meet all needs. If a service is not to be available to all, at every level of need, then it will be necessary to target those in most need.

Given a knowledge of its precise market segments the department can position itself, that is it can decide what sort of service it is going to provide for the groups that it services. Positioning, for example, will involve deciding on the quality of service. The positions adopted by newly developing services such as economic development will vary most widely because professions with uniform approaches have not yet gained control of the service. The strategic position of the service can be understood by seeing it as the answer to the question:

> What is it that differentiates our service approach in this authority from that of others?

Determining the position that the authority will take will involve analysing the key dimensions along which the service may vary. The authority will then need to decide what position it will take relative to these dimensions. In the case of housing, for example, two key dimensions might be:

- ▽ The authority acting as a major provider or the authority playing a predominantly enabling role.
- ▽ The authority providing a wide or a narrow range of services.

The combination of these two dimensions would give a categorisations of differently positioned housing departments.

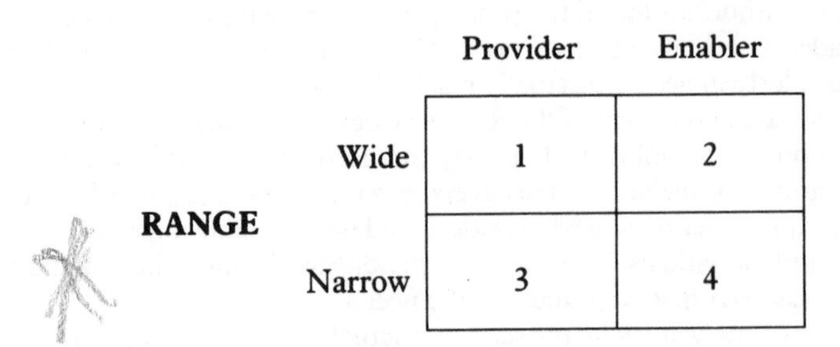

Figure 7.1. Provision

This analysis would give four positions that could be adopted by housing departments, from a totally self-contained service in box 1 to, perhaps, only trying to persuade others to find homes for the homeless in box 4. Similar positional analysis could be conducted by other services, given the development of appropriate dimensions for the analysis of position.

Positioning the service therefore involves:

▽ Determining the key dimensions along which the service to be provided may vary.
▽ Determining the position that the authority wishes to take on each service dimension.
▽ Determining the present position.
▽ Determining the action that needs to be taken to re-position the service if necessary, the barriers that will be faced and how they might be overcome.

The key dimension may be seen as centralisation as opposed to decentralisation, with the authority seeing itself as highly centralised when it wants to be decentralised. The authority will then need to determine what action is necessary to move to greater decentralisation. The degree of choice that is open to authorities in deciding on the pattern of service that they will provide is large. Statute provides a strong framework as regards the services that must be provided but there is relatively little said on the actual form that those services should take.

The market mix

The market mix is the set of factors that the service may manipulate in order to satisfy the market — notably product, price, promotion and place. For different services the mix will vary and certain components of it will be more important than others. The development of a service marketing strategy is largely the determination of the proper approach to the marketing mix.

PRODUCT

The service product may vary along a number of dimensions. We have already discussed the particular character of services, such as the involvement of the consumer in the production process, but there are also characteristics of the services provided by local authorities that follow from the fact that they are public services. The following are of particular significance.

- ▽ Collective as against individual consumption. Some services are clearly consumed by individual, separately identifiable consumers — housing and education are obvious examples. In other cases there are individual consumers but they may be hard to identify, as in the case of road usage. Other services are necessarily consumed by all, such as environmental protection or planning services. Marketing is more easily applicable to individual than collective services.
- ▽ Positive or remedial. Some services such as leisure or education are positive goods, that can be valued for their own sakes. Others such as fire, police or some social services are necessary to remedy ills of one sort or another. In an ideal world we would not need the latter type of service.
- ▽ Control or support. Some services are intended to give the authority control over the local environment, such as licensing or development control. Others have the function of developing the local area or its people such as education.
- ▽ Compulsory or voluntary — people are forced to receive certain of the services of the local authority such as education, others, such as leisure services, they are free to use or not as they choose.
- ▽ Mandatory or discretionary. Some services are tightly governed by statute, in other cases legislation is loose and largely enabling.

Different services, and the individual products that fall within them, will vary along these dimensions. Services could be scaled on these and other relevant dimensions, in order to determine the appropriate approach to pricing, promotion and service delivery. So, for example we may compare education and economic development:

Education	**Economic development**
Individual	Collective
Normally positive	Remedial
Support	Support
Compulsory	Mostly voluntary
Mandatory	Discretionary

In considering this product analysis the authority would, for example be less likely to price mandatory, compulsory, positive services than individual, voluntary, collective ones. The channels of distribution for individual, voluntary would be quite different from those for collective, compulsory ones, as would the approach to promotion.

The Government has introduced legislation that will make it compulsory for the authority to compete for the right to provide services by the use of its own directly employed labour. this requirement will apply to:

- ▽ Refuse collection.
- ▽ Street cleaning.
- ▽ Catering.
- ▽ Cleaning of buildings.
- ▽ Grounds maintenance.
- ▽ Vehicle maintenance.
- ▽ Management of leisure facilities.

Other services may be added to this list in the future. If they are to be able to put services out to tender, authorities must be able to define clearly the service that they want to be delivered. Detailed analysis of the service product will play a much greater part in the management of the local authority in the future. Services are increasingly likely to be delivered on a quasi-contractual basis. The 'contract' states the specific services that consumers can expect to receive. The contract will also involve notions of the targets that are to be met, for example the time limits for dealing with planning applications. Contract-based provision depends upon clarifying the product that is to be delivered. Essentially services will be trying to say to those they serve: 'Here is a definition of the service that you are supposed to receive, its characteristics and the benefits that it is supposed to yield'.

PRICE

As we have seen local authorities make great use of charging as a means of paying for services. In a small number of cases, notably primary and secondary education, charging is almost completely prohibited, but many services for which there is an identifiable client are priced. The Government and the Audit Commission have recommended more use of charging, and less subsidisation of cost. The range of services for which charges can be levied is wide: council housing, further education courses, trade refuse, leisure facilities, planning permission, car parks, meals-on-wheels, home helps and many others.

But the case for charging is not self-evident, and the alternative of unpriced services may be a perfectly proper and sensible approach. Whether charges should be levied and at what rate will depend upon:

- ▽ Whether the consumer of the service can be identified.
- ▽ The reason for pricing, for example pricing may be used to limit take-up.
- ▽ The ability of the consumer to pay.
- ▽ Whether pricing the service would lead to those who would most benefit from the service not to use it.
- ▽ The costs of collecting charges.
- ▽ The effect that charging will have on the relationship between the provider and the client.

In order to be able to price services effectively the authority will need a close knowledge of unit costs, and the determinants of variations in the cost of delivering services. There is an increasing need for authorities to be able to price their services accurately. The introduction of competitive tendering requires the trading unit to be able to charge the client department for the provision of a service. The need to co-operate with other agencies in the provision of services and to be able to recoup costs on the basis of usage also requires more accurate costing. There are inter-authority payments or the use of services, for example for education or police. The growth of special and supplementary grants requires authorities to be able to identify costs accurately in order to make bids. Delegated finance in the education service will require detailed knowledge of the structure of school costs. The less self sufficient the authority the more it will need to be able to price accurately.

Pricing is a key tool in managing local authority services. If there is to be the development of a greater use of cost centres there will be a need for cost centre managers to be able to cost their work effectively. It will not be possible to price all aspects of local authority services, and even if it is the price may not be chargeable. The reason that services are provided in the public sector is largely that they are not amenable to market pricing. Price information is not the only data on which we will make decisions about services and their distribution. But price considerations are crucial in allowing us to see what opportunities we forego by using our resources, whether formally priced or not, in one way rather than another. When we use money in one way we close off a whole range of other possible options.

PROMOTION

The traditional approach of local authorities has almost been to conceal services from the public, not actively to promote them. Buildings are often difficult to find, staff difficult to recognise as working for, and services not identified as being provided by, the local authority. Promotion is significant because the way that the service is presented to the public is part of the service that people receive. The services that are being delivered are often intangible and it is necessary to make the way that they are presented as tangible as possible. If people are not seen to be doing a job it may that that people will feel that the job is not being done. In one authority public satisfaction with street cleaning declined when the service was mechanised, even though standards were not thought to have declined, because people no longer actually saw the work being done. Faced with such perceptions, authorities might try to make their street cleaning vehicles more visible, change cleaning rotas, or use manual rather than mechanical methods in sensitive areas. Promotion of services involves making as clear as possible the service that is being delivered. The promotion of the service is part of the service delivery process, not something that can take place separately.

The need for promotion will vary with the nature of the service being considered. The promotion of services is most important when:

- ▽ The service will not be properly used if it is not fully understood.
- ▽ The service is new.
- ▽ Clients are likely to be ignorant of the service.
- ▽ Cost-effectiveness depends upon high usage.
- ▽ Significant changes are being made to the nature of the service.

Specialist services are likely to be poorly used if client groups do not understand or know about the service. Environmental health services fall into this category. They provide a range of specialist services, for example on pollution, that are ill-understood. The trading standards department, with its specialist skills in the analysis of consumer goods, is another example. New services require promotion if they are to succeed, for in the case of tourism and economic development services.

Promotion of services to groups that are likely to be ignorant of them, or perhaps afraid or ashamed to use them, is a means of ensuring that services reach the people for whom they are intended. People who belong to ethnic minority groups may not find out about services unless there is promotional material available in languages other than English. A number of authorities provide such materials, though smaller groups, such as Chinese people, are not well catered for. Authorities also need to consider how they can reach other groups of people in need, who may not know what services are available, such as single parent families or old people. The authority may also want to promote other government services for its own advantage. Studies have shown that those failing to claim benefit entitlements are likely to fall into rent arrears. The authority will therefore gain by supporting claimants. The promotional strategy must also involve a consideration of the links between services in providing for particular groups. It is not only the social services department that needs to promote its services to the old, but also housing, education, the police, environmental health and libraries amongst others.

The authority may make economies of scale in the provision of some services, and promotion will be important in increasing usage and take-up. Public transport will obviously be more efficient the more people use it. Promotion may be used to increase off-peak usage. It will also be necessary to be sure that people are aware of changes to the availability or character of services, for example changes in the availability of grants for housing improvement or changes in the pattern of adult education.

The requirements of competitive tendering make it necessary for the authority to promote its services to other authorities and other public sector bodies for which it can do work. Under the provisions of the Local Government (Goods and Services) Act 1970 local authorities can work for certain specified bodies. The introduction of competitive tendering and internal trading in the Local Government Planning and Land Act 1980, and the Local Government Act 1988 has made it necessary for authorities to look to broaden their base of operations in order to be able to compete more effectively. Some authorities have done work for Family Practitioner Committees or for universities. Even within the increasing constraints of legislation it is possible to expand the base of operations. One of the crucial marketing decisions for direct service organisations in the future is whether to adopt a defensive or an expansionist market strategy.

PLACE

Most local authority services are delivered through decentralised institutions such as schools, residential homes, colleges, libraries, museums and works depots. Some of these establishments have great autonomy, for example colleges of further education. Most make use of central local authority facilities for buying materials and supplies, for administrative support, and for expert advice. Such decentralisation, combining centralisation and decentralisation, can allow the authority to gain economies both of scale and scope. The present moves for the decentralisation of financial responsibility to schools and colleges creates the danger that efficient patterns of organisation will be lost.

But the question of how the channels of service delivery should be organised is more than a matter of how much autonomy should be granted to local institutions. Two further questions must be considered:

- ▽ How much should the local authority plan a service as a system?
- ▽ How integrated should the distribution of different services be?

Much of the activity of local government has been system level planning, the development of an integrated and co-ordinated pattern of service delivery. This system planning role has been strong in education, social services, transportation, planning and housing. In the last ten years there has grown up a renewed faith in the power of unregulated market forces to determine the pattern of service. The most recent example is the proposal to introduce open enrolments in schools so that parents can choose to send their child to a school as long as it has the physical space.

Local authority services have traditionally been distributed through separately organised departments. In the last decade there have been attempts to break down the separateness in service delivery systems. The trend to decentralisation in many authorities is coupled with an attempt to bring together services in a neighbourhood office, particularly through the integration of social services and housing. Other authorities have attempted to develop co-terminous boundaries for services in order to improve the chances for integrated working. Westminster City Council has adopted one stop shopping in order to prevent people being shunted from department to department. Authorities have attempted to develop the joint use of facilities especially through the use of schools for leisure activities outside school hours. These developments all recognise the need for authorities to consider the channels of distribution of services across services as well as within services.

The problems of service distribution are greater in rural than urban areas. Scottish and Welsh authorities, especially, face the difficulty of sparcity of population. Offices may be a long way from outlying villages. Distribution of services is obviously costly in such services, and there is often a need for circulating services, such as mobile libraries. The authority may make use of other facilities such as Post Offices for the distribution of information. New technology may help to overcome some of the problems of sparcity. In one county the education department has been experimenting with distance learning packages in order to maintain sixth-form provision in small schools. Other authorities have experimented with 'cluster' schools where a number of schools in adjacent villages are linked together and served by a common staff. Distribution is a difficult problem for local authorities. The fact that many of the products that it produces are services means that it is difficult to maintain inventories. There are examples of inventory like processes, such as the employment of central pools of supply teachers, but more commonly the authority cannot staff up to meet peaks of demand. It is harder to ensure a match of supply and demand, not only because of shortages but because the distribution of services is more difficult than that of material goods.

Conclusion

Local authority services differ widely from one another and require different marketing strategies. In some cases we compel usage; in others we try to restrict it; and in others we try to promote it. Some goods are beneficial, others for control, and others still are intended to make good social or environmental ills. Some goods are used collectively and others by identifiable individuals. The purposes of, and approach to, marketing will depend upon the nature of the service. It may be active promotion or it may be negative demarketing. Careful analysis is needed of the nature of the product and who it is being designed for, if a clear marketing strategy is to be developed.

Questions and exercises

▲ *1. Try to make as detailed a list as possible of the services that your authority provides.*

▲ *2. Which of the services that the department provides are provided to individual users?*

▲ *3. Which services that the department provides are provided for the community as a whole?*

▲ *4. Consider a service of the authority or a component of a service. Which is the most appropriate position to adopt:*
Mass marketing
Differentiated marketing
Focused marketing

▲ *5. How might the service that you provide contribute to the well-being of:*
Children
Old people
Women
Unemployed people
Young people
Single parents
Homeless people
Mothers with young children
People with disabilities

▲ *6. Try to list the groups that fall into the following categories in the case of your service.*
Recipients
Direct beneficiaries
Indirect beneficiaries
Advocates

▲ *7. Who is affected negatively by your service?*

▲ *8. What means do you use to determine need for your service?*

▲ *9. What is it that differentiates the service that you provide from that provided by other authorities?*

▲ *10. In considering the positioning of your service:*
What are the dimensions along which your service can vary?
What position do you presently take on each?
What is your desired position?
How might the gap be closed?

▲ *11. What are the problems that you face in distributing your service?*

8 The internal market

Key points

- ▲ *The authority as an internal market.*
- ▲ *Growing complexity and rising standards.*
- ▲ *The chain of value – the contribution of secondary services to quality.*
- ▲ *The aspects of the contribution of secondary services to quality:*
  - *materials*
  - *staff*
  - *logistics*
  - *systems*
  - *information*
  - *property*
- ▲ *Internal segments – the politicians and the other departments.*
- ▲ *The position of secondary services – control, coordination and support.*
- ▲ *Determining the nature of the individual services.*
- ▲ *Pricing within the authority.*
- ▲ *Promotion of secondary services within the authority.*
- ▲ *Delegation and decentralisation of secondary services.*

Local authorities must not only consider the ways that they market the services they produce to the users or consumers, they must also be viewed as internal markets. This is so for two reasons. First, the local authority is a highly differentiated organisation in which either is extensive internal trading and exchange or services. Second, the fact that the local authority provides services rather than material products means that the service that is provided cannot be separated from the people who provide it. It is therefore necessary for those who provide services to be clear on the nature of the service and on the organisation's strategy. This mean that the local authority must market its services not only to users but also to its staff. In a services organisation the attutide and actions of the front-line staff will have a direct impact on the experience of the consumer or user. The process of developing a clear understanding of their position and the service that they are intended to provide will involve marketing techniques.

Internal training

The local authority is a set of units engaged in internal trading. Individuals, groups and departments are part of a larger unit of community government that is organised to produce a total approach, not just a range of individual services. Some services are more tightly coupled than others, and the effect of one may depend upon the performance of another. Education and social services have very strong links with one another in the provision of education for pupils and students who have mental and physical disabilities. Planning and transportation must work closely together in the provision of road systems. Police and fire services must work together in dealing with emergencies. Housing and social services must work together in providing proper housing for the elderly. Few of the services that a local authority operates can be treated in a completely isolated fashion.

Traditionally local authorities were organised in a highly departmental fashion, with each service profession being organised into its own separate department such as engineering, planning or housing. Departments had as little to do with each other as possible, preferring automony and avoiding co-operative working. As the world became more complex, and problems no longer fell into neat departmental catagories, the autonomous approach became less appropriate. Dealing with inner city deprivation and dereliction, for example is clearly not the preserve of a single department. The causes of social problems are complex and demand complex solutions. New functions are being developed that do not fit into traditional professional categories. Traditional departmental approaches do not cope well with the more complex problems that local authorities now face. The need for more integrated working was recognised in the corporate management and corporate planning movement of the 1970s.

The corporate movement argued that the need for integrated working in local government should be recognised in the management structures and systems of local authorities. Variants of the approach were recommended by the Bains Report, the Paterson Report and many others. After reorganisation in 1974, most authorities adopted a corporate approach with varying degrees of enthusiasm. The corporate approach to managing local authorities involved the appointment of chief executives and personnel officers, the establishment of policy committees and management teams and, less frequently directorate systems and programme committees. Corporate systems involved research and intelligence and annual policy and budgeting procedures. The initial enthusiasm for fully blown corporate systems quickly waned. But the general approach has become part of the established working of the majority of authorities. The recent, more partial, recognition of the consumer perspective, implies a more widely corporate approach that recognises the need for integration at the point of delivery. The corporate management movement of the 1970s focused on the centre of the authority and aimed at internal integration. The new corporatism needs to be focused on the experiences of the consumers, ensuring that the experience they have of the authority is coherent.

The corporate approach to the client means managing his or her experience, not structuring that experience to fit the prior, and possibly irrelevant, boundaries of the organisation. Consumer need and choice should determine how the organisation works, not the organisation limit consumer experience. Different departments may be dependant on one another in delivering service. Some departments only exist to serve the departments that actually deliver services to the client. Central departments such as treasurers, personnel, law and computing exist largely to provide professional support services to those who actually deliver services to the client. Catering, cleaning, transport and other ancillary services only exist to provide support to the direct service providers. They have no justification in themselves. The actual delivery of service depends upon a range of co-ordinating, support and control functions. These various secondary services only have meaning within the context of the delivery of primary services. The obvious danger is that the organisation looks inward not outward, that secondary services dominate at the expense of the actual delivery of service to the public.

Relationships between these support services and those dealing directly with the public are changing for two reasons. First, support services are becoming more complex, and professional standards are rising. Technological advance enables support services to become more sophisticated, and to respond more quickly to need. Even labour intensive activities, such as cleaning and catering have changed as a result of the development of cleaning machinery and new approaches to the preparation of food. The second change is the development of competitive tendering and trading. The traditional assumption has been that in the main, support services will be supplied by directly employed labour. The decision has been that the authority will make or produce the service itself rather than purchase it on the market. Central government pressure is forcing local authorities to compete with external contractors if they wish to win the right to provide services through directly employed staff. Local authorities are moving towards being contracting organisations. Internal relations between support services and those delivering service to the public are having to be established on a contractual basis.

The introduction of competitive tendering and the search for more efficient patterns of working is leading those involved in the delivery of service to question the cost of support services. As local authorities move towards the establishment of cost centre management, for example with the delegation of finance to schools, then operational officers, headteachers and others are coming to question the way in which the costs of central establishment functions are charged out to them. Simple means of allocation, such as basing the charge on the size of the budget or the number of people employed in likely to be questioned because they may bear no relationship to the actual use or value of the central service.

The chain of service value

We should establish support services so that they contribute to the value of the experience that the client gets. There is no point in having a highly efficient financial system if it is not helping the primary service departments to deliver better service. The purpose of the secondary service is to enable a better service to be delivered to the public. They are part of the chain of value that run from the policy decision to develop a particular service to the actual delivery. The value added may be illustrated by using the example of the personnel function and considering how the services that it provides may contribute to the experience of the ultimate consumer.

Personnel Function Value Chains

Function	Contribution to Value
Recruitment	Ensuring that the appropriate parts of the labour market is reached by the recruitment process
Selection	Ensuring that the best staff are selected
Training	Developing the capacity of staff to operate effectively
Industrial Relations	Preventing breakdowns in service
Planning	Ensuring that there will be staff to provide the service effectively in the future

Welfare	Motivating staff to provide good service
Reward Systems	Retaining good staff and providing incentive

In the case of personnel the chain of quality linking the secondary service to the experience of the client or consumer will be through the staff of the primary service. Other secondary services need to be clear on the route from the functions that they provide to the ultimate consumer of the service.

Of course, the processes involved are more complex than this in large, highly differentiated organisations. But the organisation is not kept going for its own sake. Secondary services contribute to the quality of the service that the consumer receives through efficient internal organisational systems. It is easy for those services to take on a life of their own, for example, collecting information or statistics because they 'have always done so'. There needs to be continual monitoring and audit of secondary services to ensure that they are still making an effective contribution to the experience of the client.

The contribution of secondary services

Secondary services can determine the extent to which those involved in service delivery are able to deliver an effective service. Each support group, section or department must determine its mission by analysing how best it can contribute to the experience of the user. We may think of support services as providing a number of types of contribution to the quality of service:

▽ Materials quality — purchasing and supplies departments provide quality materials either for the direct provision of service, for example, school exercise books or aids for daily living, or indirectly, for example office equipment. The authority needs to be sure that it is more effective to purchase through an internal supplies department rather than, for example, allowing cost centre managers to make their own purchasing arrangements.

▽ Staff quality — the contribution of the personnel function is the management of human resources to ensure that the right people are hired, that they are properly trained and deployed, and that they are motivated to produce good service.

▽ Logistics quality — ensuring that staff and materials come together as necessary, requiring attention to transport and the physical siting of services.

▽ Systems quality — the design and maintenance of efficient office and computing systems.

▽ Information quality — ensuring that primary service departments get the right information at the right time to allow them to control and coordinate services.

▽ Property quality — management of the real estate of the authority so that the service departments have an effective environment in which to work.

The local authority as a complex organisation involves a series of streams, of staff, materials, finance and information, amongst others that come together in the final service delivery.

Internal segmentation

The process of market segmentation is different when we are considering the organisation as an internal market. It is not easy for departments serving each other to determine who the client is. This is partly because local authorities are political organisations and those at the centre of the authority must look both towards the politicans as well as towards those who are delivering services. There may well be a tension between the sort of information that the elected members want and the sort of activity that is necessary to get the day-to-day work of the authority done. The first division within the authority itself then is that between those who primarily serve members and those who serve other officers. Elected members can in turn be segmented into different interest groupings on the basis of:

- ▽ Personal policy interests.
- ▽ Committee membership.
- ▽ Position in the party group.
- ▽ Constituency interest.

In each case different systems will be needed for servicing members in order to meet their different interests. For example, it will be necessary to have information based on wards if some of the questions of constituents are to be answered.

The second segment is the officer structure. This is most obviously further segmented on a departmental basis. Central departments will often have specific officers designated for liaison with individual service departments. The position that secondary service departments adopt towards primary services may vary along three dimensions:

- ▽ Control — central departments may control the detailed operation of others. The finance department will lay down financial rules and regulations, the personnel department may control the recruitment of staff, the materials used may be controlled through the supplies, and the computer department may control the information technology strategy of departments.
- ▽ Co-ordination — it may be necessary to co-ordinate the work of departments, for example in caring for client groups that cross the boundaries of individual departments.
- ▽ Support — providing back-up and ancillary services as necessary.

The position adopted by secondary departments will often be a combination of control, co-ordination and support, which may not be clear to the primary service department.

The internal market mix

There is a need for the market mix to operate within the authority in the dealing between departments and with the elected members as there is in dealing with the delivery of services to client. Their services that one part of the organisation supplies to another are products that carry a price, either explicitly or implicitly, that need to be promoted and that must be appropriately distributed. Marketing principles can be applied to these various processes as they operate within the organisation.

SUPPORT SERVICES AS INTERNAL PRODUCTS

If it is difficult to be precise about primary service products, it is even more difficult to define the products that secondary service producers provide to direct providers of service. The problem is less difficult for material services, such as catering, transport, purchasing and computing, where fairly precise specification is possible.

The difficulties are greater with less tangible secondary services. Professional services offering advice and support will always have an element of vagueness about them. Certainly it is not always apparent to client departments what purpose professional support departments serve. Resentment and dissatisfaction with the service received from support departments is common. The difficulties arise from three principle sources:

▽ Confusion and uncertainty about the precise role of the support department. It is not always clear why rules and regulations exist or why a central department is requiring information. It may not be obvious who should be contacted in a particular case. These problems arise particularly for those who work in schools, residential homes, branch libraries and other direct service units, who find it particularly difficult to develop a clear picture of the role of central departments and offices. Part of the marketing role for central services and offices. Part of the marketing role for central services departments is ensuring that there are clear points of contact for service delivery units, and that central staff are known to those they serve.
▽ The perceived insensitivity of central departments to the needs of their clients. Information is often seen as arriving too late to be relevant or being presented in a way that makes it unuseable. Central departments need to spend more time determining the needs of client departments, which will involve market research.
▽ The combination of control and support can lead to confused messages. Finance, legal and personnel departments need to ensure that standing orders, financial regulations, statute and other rules are adhered to, and must audit to ensure financial probity and efficiency. Such control functions may easily become confused with support functions such as advice or the provision of management information.

Central service departments need to be precise about what service they are providing to their client department and why they are providing it. It will always be valuable to ask the question. 'Would other departments continue to use our service if they were not forced to?'

Central departments therefore need to design the service they provide so that it meets the need of the client department. The characteristics to be considered will vary with the specific service. In the case of computer services for example one might want to consider:

▽ Accuracy — the computer should provide more accurate information than manual systems.
▽ Speed — computerised information should be available at least as quickly as would manually produced information.
▽ Volume — the computer system should be able to deal with large amounts of information and to be capable of being extended if necessary.

- ▽ Detail — the computer should provide information at the appropriate level of detail.
- ▽ Adaptable — a computer system should be able to respond to changing need.
- ▽ Accessible — information should be easily retrievable from the computer.
- ▽ Interactive — the user should be able to interrogate the system.
- ▽ Reliable — free from error and not subject to breakdown.
- ▽ Secure — should protect sensitive information.
- ▽ Cost effective — should provide value for money.

Other central services will have their own dimensions that will need to be considered in designing the service to be delivered to client departments.

Product specifications need to be worked out with those who are to use the product. A common experience is that sytems are developed that do not meet client department needs because client departments have not adequately involved themselves or been consulted. For example, it is common to find officers in client departments keeping their own financial accounts because they find the financial information provided by the finance department to be inadequate, because it comes too late, or is not in the form that is needed, or simply because staff have never been trained to intepret it. The failure is on both sides. Support departments do not make enough effort to find out what the client needs and the client department does not work hard enough at understanding and making clear its own needs. It is often easier to complain about the other department's failing than to do anything about it.

The growth of internal trading — of the local authority as an internal market — requires a greater emphasis upon marketing within the local authority. A major priority for the future is the development of clear services specifications not only for those services that are to be subject to competitive tendering but also for the internal support services of the authority. As cost centre management becomes more common the managers of primary services will come to demand much clearer information on the services that they are being provided by secondary services.

Price

Service delivery departments are charged from the services that they receive from central support departments through the central establishment charge. The prices charged for central services are seen as a great source of complaint for three reasons:

- ▽ The charges levied are often seen as being too high.
- ▽ The allocation of charges between departments may be seen as unfair.
- ▽ The methods used to determine charges may be seen as inappropriate.

No doubt some of this complaint is simply the result of the natural tendency for people not to like paying their bills for the very good reason that they will have less money left when they have done so. Nor is the complaint about the allocation of central establishment charges simply a local authority or public sector phenomenon. It is a feature just as much of the private sector and the same arguments are made about the procedures used being unfair or inappropriate. There is no universal, foolproof, method of allocating overhead costs.

The sort of internal transfer pricing systems that should be used depends upon:

- ▽ The nature of the organisation involved and particularly the degree of cooperation and diversity that is involved in its activity.
- ▽ The purposes of the organisation.

The more diversified the organisation, the more transfers will be necessary between its components parts. If transfers are priced, then diversification will lead to an extensive process of internal transfer payments, which is quite feasible but is also time-consuming, especially when the paths are indirect. The complexity is obvious when we consider those activities that are subject to competitive tendering using services that are themselves required to compete. The more diversified the organisation the more complex the internal pricing system will be.

When the organisation has multiple purposes rather than a single purpose, then inter-departmental transfers will be complex. The simpler the organisation, and the more it is producing a single final product, the less complex the transfer pricing system. It is easier to decide on the internal pricing system if the organisation has a single purpose such as maximising profit or income. In the local authority purposes will increasingly come into conflict, as one part of the organisation is required to make a surplus where another is oriented to service. The direct service organisation, supplying catering or vehicle maintenance may want to charge a high price where it can, especially if the surplus can be shared by the staff. The result may simply be that less money is available to provide direct services to the public.

Different approaches to internal pricing are appropriate in different circumstances and for different purposes. There are four methods of internal pricing:

- ▽ Recharge at actual cost.
- ▽ Recharge at standard cost.
- ▽ Recharge at market price.
- ▽ Recharge at a negotiated price.

Actual cost is the normal basis for charging inside the local authority. The actual costs of running central services are re-allocated on a formula basis, with allocations determined by variables such as staff numbers, budgets or floor area. In the case of trading services subject to competitive tendering internal charging will increasingly be on the basis of standard costs. Market price is most useful when there is a market in the particular service and when the department or unit sells its services both within and outside the organisation. Negotiated prices might be used for a variety of purposes, for example to encourage use or to help a section of the organisation facing difficulty.

The widespread development of competitive tendering and internal trading will lead to greater pressure for accurate internal pricing systems. Those parts of the authority that must operate as direct service organisations, competing and operating trading accounts, will be concerned that they do not bear excessive central costs. Though central establishment charges are only a small part of the total cost of a direct service organisation, they will be important in a tightly competitive market. They are also an element of the direct service managers costs that are outside his or her control.

The Chartered Institute of Public Finance and Accounting recommends full internal reallocation of costs for two reasons:

> Firstly, it makes (or it should make) an authority's managers look carefully at the total resources that the authority uses. In this context, the cost of support services is just as much a cost of the service as direct expenditure and it is the direct services to the public that benefit from the back-up of support services. . . . It follows that unless each service to the public is charged with its fair share support services, there will be no restraint on the demand for support services. . . . Second, full and consistent allocation is essential because it greatly increases the possibility of comparing on a logical basis different authorities costs. (CIPFA, Support Services — Value For Money? p. 13).

But as the Audit Commission argues the method of allocation must be fair:

> Although there are marked variations in the resources used by treasurers to give similar services to departments, this is not reflected in recharges which are based upon block allocations of time to services. More accountable methods of recharge are needed, not just to DLO's and newly created subsidiaries, but more widely in order to maximise the potential for service providers to influence their own budgets (although of course their influence is necessarily limited in issues of financial control). Otherwise as the Commission found in its study of housing management, recharges are likely to be seen as the dumping on services of expenditure over which they have no control, and which they cannot relate to the quality of service provided.

The pressures of trading, competitive tendering and financial constraints are leading authorities to examine closely their method of recharging centrally provided services.

It is important that the appropriate method of internal pricing is used if resources are not to be misallocated within the authority. If, for example, legal services are provided free it may well be that there are too many prosecutions and that officers adopt legalistic approaches simply because legal services are available. It is also necessary that the method of determining the use of central services is not too complex. Detailed timesheets, for example may be a costly method compared with departments opting into a particular level of service at the beginning of the year.

Promotion within the authority

Relations between departments within the local authority are often poor, each wishes to be independent and views others with suspicion. There is often considerable ignorance about other departments even if they have to work closely together. The traditions of different departments based upon different professional backgrounds makes communication difficult. The result is that the service delivered by the secondary service department may not be the service that the client department wants. Elected members also have only a limited knowledge of what the various departments and sections of the authority do. Departments need a promotion strategy that will help elected members and other departments to relate effectively to them. There are a number of methods of ensuring that members and other departments are aware of the nature of a department's or section's activities:

- ▽ Written material
- ▽ Induction and briefing
- ▽ Training courses

As internal trading develops and as changes such as the delegation of finance to schools gathers pace there will be an increasing need for secondary service departments to develop an effective promotional strategy.

Place

Local authorities are highly dispersed organisations, made up of many institutions and individual units. The main question that arises in the organisation of channels of distribution of services within the organisation are:

- ▽ How much should the authority decentralised to the various institutions charged with the local delivery of service?
- ▽ How much should the local authority delegate to individual service departments?

Decentralisation has been increasing. Schools, residential homes and other units have been given more automony over the way that they control their budgets. In some authorities, such as Solihull and Cambridgeshire, there have already been attempts to delegate budgets to schools, and the Education Reform Act 1988 is to require the delegation of finance to all schools of 200 pupils or over. Other departments have been experimenting with decentralisation of control over resources. Some authorities are investigating the possibility of moving wholly to a management system based on cost centres with a good deal of automony over their budgets. Decentralisation of the control of resources is intended to provide an incentive for the more efficient use of resources, and the development of greater accountability.

The second question is how much should the authority decentralise control of resources and support services to individual departments rather than operate on a centralised basis. Should departments rely on a central personnel or financial function or have their own financial and legal capacity? In part this is a question of size; larger departments may generate enough work to justify having their own independent capacity, whereas smaller departments will need to expect support of a central department and may benefit from economies of scale. The move to internal trading in local authorities is tending to lead to the decentralisation of some functions. In St Helens Borough Council the personnel department has begun to operate on a trading basis at the same time decentralising certain work:

> In 1986 the personnel section underwent restructuring and devolved all the purely administrative functions (together with the relevant staff) to the service departments. The central unit was then left with a few specialist functions — manpower planning, recruitment, industrial relations, training and employment initiatives. Each of these operates as far as possible on a consultancy basis to the line manager. . . . (Local Government Chronicle, 7 August 1987)

In other cases, for example transport, the development of internal trading is likely to lead to greater concentration. The Audit Commission's study of vehicle fleet management, for example argued for:

> Centralised managerial control in most if not all cases. . .

finding that this allowed:

- ▽ Pooling arrangements.
- ▽ The right balance of ownership and spot and contract hiring.
- ▽ Minimisation of transport overheads.
- ▽ Clearer managerial accountability.
- ▽ Clarification of the costs of owning and running vehicles.

Many authorities have also been introducing more centralised control and management of property. The tendency is to decentralise the less tangible support services and to centralise and integrate the management of the more tangible support services such as property and transport. The less easy it is to specify a service and to control its quality, the more it makes sense to provide that service by employing one's own staff rather than purchasing it from elsewhere, whether the open market or another department in the organisation. The more nebulous the service the more direct managerial control is needed.

There will always be a tension between the centralised and the decentralised control of resources in the local authority. Economies of scale and scope will tend to lead to centralisation, but the notion of the primacy of the client service will tend to lead to decentralisation. The more tangible the product or service involved the more likely it is that the centralisation of the service will be the more efficient way to organise because the service can be closely specified and economies of scale reaped. The less tangible the service the more appropriate is decentralised control. Peters and Waterman capture the tension that is involved in the organisation of channels of service distribution and control within the organisation in their finding that excellent organisations exhibit 'simultaneous loose–tight properties'.

Conclusion

Local authorities are developing as explicit internal markets under the pressure of government and legislation, shortage of resources, the desire for greater accountability and the development of new management approaches. An organisation as large as a local authority will always be an extensive internal market. There will be trading between central support and operational service departments and between different service departments. The more complex the services with which the authority is concerned the more extensive the internal trading links will be. The various departments of the authority must operate together, which requires active networking in which the concepts of the marketing perspectives will have a large part to play. The authority internally can be seen as a set of producer-client relations, and all the interactions that take place in the organisation can be analysed to determine who is the client for the service that is being provided, and what benefit is the producer of the service producing.

The internal market can be seen as a network of resource chains adding value to the service. The proper internal organisation of these chains of value becomes more important the longer the service has been established. For new services it is the product itself that is the focus of analysis. For long established products or services innovation, effectiveness and efficiency are more likely to be sought in systems of design, production and delivery. It is not much the service itself that is important, but the way that the 'service system' works. As Normann says:

> It is necessary to identify the key determinants of success in a service business and to reflect them in the management and nature of the organisation, so that a system can first be produced and subsequently maintained systematically over a long period of time.

In analysing the service we must consider the operation of the whole organisation and not simply its points of service delivery.

Questions and exercises

▲ *1. Consider a central department. What does it contribute to the quality of service? What features of service produce the contribution?*

▲ *2. Consider the contribution of support services to quality. Is the contribution effective for each of the following aspects of support:*
materials quality
staff quality
logistics quality
systems quality
information quality
property quality

▲ *3. For each support service, what aspects of the service are intended for:*
control
co-ordination
support

▲ *4. What aspects of central services would be unlikely to be used if services departments were allowed a choice?*

▲ *5. What are the important characteristics of the support service that you provide or that is provided to you? For example, is it speed of response, accuracy or what?*

▲ *6. Which is the most appropriate form of pricing for various support services?*

	Actual Cost	*Standard Cost*	*Market Cost*	*Negotiated Cost*
Finance				
Legal services				
Personnel services				
Management services				
Computer services				
Building maintenance				
Estates services				
Other				

▲ *7. Which support services should be delegated more to departments in local authorities?*

9 Conclusion

Local authorities provide services rather than manufactured products. The crucial link that determines the quality of the service that the user experiences is the link with the individual member of staff or the staff group that provides the service. This will be more so the more the consumer and the producer must interact to make the service happen. It is at the boundary of the organisation that the crucial processes of service production take place. It is at the boundary of the organisation also that breakdowns in service delivery are most likely to happen. The quality of staff is crucial to the quality of the service that the customer receives. But the ability of those working at the boundary of the organisation in contact with the public will not be determined not only by their own efforts but also the way that the whole organisation works to support them. We need to consider how the back-line of the organisation contributes to front-line services. The local authority is not like a manufacturing organisation that makes its product and then distributes it. In the case of services the process is simultaneous. The staff who produce the service are also crucial in marketing it.

The fact that staff in service organisations are the key to the consumer's experience means that the authority must be sure that staff have a clear understanding of their roles and responsibilities and the way that their actions influence the consumer's experience. In the case of manufacturing industry much of the control of the activities of the workforce can be incorporated into the technology. In labour intensive services such technologically based control is not possible. Rather the authority must operate through generating understanding of the role that they are to play and commitment to it. The authority, that is, must market the service to the staff.

Centralisation or decentralisation

A small number of local authorities have set up marketing departments in the attempt to develop a more customer orientated approach to the delivery of local services. But introducing a marketing perspective into the local authority does not necessarily mean appointing specialist staff and setting up specialist departments. The argument of this book has been that local authorities may have something to learn from the introduction of a marketing perpsective but also that, because they deliver services and because they are publicly accountable organisations, the form that any marketing approach needs to take is different. The pattern of involvement of the staff with the public in the production of a service strongly suggests a decentralised approach to marketing. The danger of a marketing department is that it leads to the assumption that the development of responsive service is the responsibility of a centralised department.

The experience that the consumer has will be determined at the edge of the organisation and that is where the majority of the marketing effort will need to take place. The process of marketing cannot be separated from the process of service delivery so there must be constant attention to marketing in the course of actually providing the service. Marketing will also need to be part of the service planning process and this cannot be left to central departments. It is a matter for those who must manage the service to determine the form that it should take in collaboration with those who will use it.

Local authorities, if they are to adopt a marketing perspective, need to do so on a decentralised, and non-professional basis. The power needs to lie with the operational manager. Each department needs to consider how the concepts of marketing apply to its own service. This is not to say that there can be no purpose in a centralised marketing section, department or unit. The question is more one of what marketing functions should be carried out on a centralised, and which on a decentralised basis. We would suggest that four principles might be useful in making this decision:

- ▽ That a marketing function is more likely to be provided on a centralised basis when it involves highly specialist skills, for example statistical ability for the development of marketing research. We would argue that these highly specialised skills will not be called for so often as to warrant the establishment of an extensive central function.
- ▽ The less the application of a marketing perspective involves a detailed knowledge of the specific service involved. This will rarely be the case because the whole point of the marketing perspective is that a close knowledge of the product and the consumer is necessary to the effectiveness of an organisation.
- ▽ When the particular aspect of marketing can be tightly specified then it will be more appropriate to establish it on a centralised basis. Thus it will be easier to operate public relations and statistical work centrally because it can be more clearly defined.
- ▽ The less easy it is to identify an individual consumer, customer or user of the service then the less important the relationship between provider and user and the more the marketing process can be separated from the point of delivery.

It would also seem highly inappropriate to establish centralised marketing departments in local authorities at a time when there is a great deal of questioning of the future of central support departments.

If marketing is to play a greater role in the way that local authorities deliver services then it is more important that those who provide the service develop a marketing perspective than that the authority appoint marketing professionals who can apply their skills to services. Marketing professionals have little experience of marketing public services and the marketing perspective cannot simply be bought into the organisation.

Conclusion

Marketing can be seen as a mixture of technique and philosophy. There are strongly developed techniques, but they are not of great significance to local authorities at this stage of development. On the other hand we have argued that the concepts of the marketing can be useful to a local authority that is concerned to develop a more public service orientation. The marketing perspective can play a small part in the development of a form of local authority that is more responsive to the needs and wishes of those to whom it provides service, but it should not be left up to the professional marketers.

Bibliography

Ajzen, I. and Fishbein, M. (1984) *Understanding Attitudes and Predicting Behaviour.* Prentice-Hall, New Jersey.

Albrecht, K. and Kemize, R. (1988) *Service America!* Dow-Jones-Irwin. Homewood, Illinois.

Arden, A. (1986–1987) *Hackney: London Borough Inquiry.*

Arnstein, S. (1969) 'A Ladder of Participation in the USA'. *Journal of the American Institute of Planners* (July).

Audit Commission (1984) *Improving Vehicle Fleet Management in Local Government.*

Audit Commission (1985) *Good Management in Local Government* (with Local Government Training Board and INLOGOV).

Audit Commission (1986) *Improving Cash Flow Managment in Local Government.*

Baddeley, S. and Dawes, N. (1986) 'Service to the Customer'. *RIPA Report* (Spring).

Baker, M. J. (1975) *Marketing: An Introductory Text.* Macmillan.

Bem, D. J. (1970) *Beliefs, Attitudes and Human Affairs.* Belmont, California.

Berelson, B., Lazarsfelt, P. and McPhee, W. N. (1954) *Voting.* Chicago, University of Chicago Press.

Beresford, P. (1987) *Good Council Guide: Wandsworth — 1978–1987.* Centre for Policy Studies.

Birkenshaw, P. (1986) *Open Government: Freedom of Information and Local Government.* Local Government Legal Society Trust.

Bovaird, A. (1981) *Review of Changing Policy in Dudley MBC.* University of Aston.

Chartered Institute of Public Finance and Accounting (LIPFA) (1986) *Support Services – Value for Money?.*

Cowell, D. (1984) *The Marketing of Services.* Heinemann.

Engel, J. F., Kollat, D. J. and Blackwell, R. D. (1973) *Consumer Behaviour.* Dryden Press, Illinois.

Department of the Environment (1981) *Service Provision and Pricing in Local Government.*

Fairlie, H. (1968) *The Life of Politics.* Methuen.

Goffman, E. (1959) *Asylums.* Harmondsworth, Penguin.

Harrison, R. (1987) *Organisation Culture and Quality of Service.* Association for Management Education and Development.

Herzberg, F. *Work and the Nature of Man.* St Albans, Staples.

Johnson, G. and Scholes K. (1984) *Exploring Corporate Strategy.* Prentice-Hall International, London.

Kesserjian, H. (1971) 'Personality and Consumer Behaviour: A Review'. *Journal of Marketing Research.* Vol. 8, 1971.

Kotler, P. (1982) *Marketing for Non-profit Organisations.* Prentice-Hall.

Landes, D. (1983) *The Revolution in Time.* Harvard University Press.

Lapiere, R. T. (1934) 'Attitudes versus Actions'. *Social Forces.* Vol. 13, pp 230–37.

Levitt, T. (1972) 'Production Line Approach to Service'. *Harvard Business Review* (September).

Lewis, N., Seneviratne, M. and Cracknell, S. (1987) *Complaints Procedures in Local Government.* University of Sheffield.

Local Government Training Board (1987) *Getting Closer to the Public.*

Miller, W. (1986) *Local Electoral Behaviour.* The Conduct of Local Authority Business (Widdicombe Report). Research Volume III.

Moran, W. R. (1973) 'Why New Products Fail'. *Journal of Advertising Research.* Vol. 13.

National Consumer Council (1987) *Measuring Up.*

National Council of Voluntary Organisations (1984) *Clients' Rights.*

Normann, R. (1984) *Services Management.* J. Wiley.

Ogilvy, D. (1987) *Confessions of an Advertising Man.* Pan.

Peters, T. J.and Waterman, R. H. (1981) *In Search of Excellence.* New York, Harper and Row.

Rhodes, R. (1987) 'Developing the Public Service Orientation'. *Local Government Studies.* Vol. 13, No. 3.

Seabrook, J. (1984) *The Idea of Neighbourhood.* Pluto.

Shostack, G. (1984) 'Designing Services that Deliver'. *Harvard Business Review.*

Shostack, G. (1977) 'Breaking Free from Product Marketing'. *Journal of Marketing.* Vol. 41, No. 2.

Stacey, M. (1976) 'The Health Services Consumer: A Sociological Misconception'. In: Stacey, M. (ed) *The Sociology of the NHS.* University of Keele (Sociological Review Monograph, 22).

Stanton, W. J. (1981) *Fundamentals of Marketing.* McGraw-Hill, New York.

Toffler, A. (1980) *The Third Wave.* New York, Collins.

Young, K. (1986) *Attitudes to Local Government.* The Conduct of Local Authority Business (Widdicombe Report). Research Volume III.

Index